Note for Librarians: A cataloguing record for this book is available from Library and Archives Canada at www.collectionscanada.ca/amicus/index-e.html

ISBN 978-1-4269-1157-6

Printed on paper with minimum 30% recycled fibre. Trafford's print shop runs on "green energy" from solar, wind and other environmentally-friendly power sources.

TRAFFORD
PUBLISHING™

Offices in Canada, USA, Ireland and UK

This book was published *on-demand* in cooperation with Trafford Publishing. On-demand publishing is a unique process and service of making a book available for retail sale to the public taking advantage of on-demand manufacturing and Internet marketing. On-demand publishing includes promotions, retail sales, manufacturing, order fulfilment, accounting and collecting royalties on behalf of the author.

Book sales for North America and international:
Trafford Publishing, 6E–2333 Government St.,
Victoria, BC v8t 4p4 CANADA
phone 250 383 6864 (toll-free 1 888 232 4444)
fax 250 383 6804; email to orders@trafford.com

Book sales in Europe:
Trafford Publishing (uk) Ltd., Enterprise House, Wistaston Road Business Centre,
Wistaston Road, Crewe, Cheshire cw2 7rp UNITED KINGDOM
phone 01270 251 396 (local rate 0845 230 9601)
facsimile 01270 254 983; orders.uk@trafford.com

Order online at:
trafford.com/04-2237

10 9 8 7 6 5 4 3 2 1

Hoover, I Spy PI

What is important is the success of an investigation.

One spy character, a professional private investigator, aka Mel Hoover Jr., can perform successful surveillance or discovery in gathering intelligence or hard to get information. Hoover is the Man! You name the case, Hoover has done it with great success, more than likely. Anywhere. Any Time. No case too small nor too large for the Hoover Investigative Agency. However, there are times you don't succeed per say, but overall, it still could be a successful investigation overall with the results obtained.

Acknowledgment

I would like to acknowledge my associates in the private sector and within law enforcement agencies and other affiliates who have assisted or encouraged me during my career as a professional private investigator all these years. Thank you!

Special Note

This book, intended for your enjoyment and information regarding the private sector, reveals the naked truth. It was written to document the only profession that has been intriguing in my life. The book, intended for entertainment to the general public and educational to the novice PI, reveals information about the private investigator, the methods, theories, and conclusions of true life cases.

Information in this book is not intended to be used for illegal purposes. The material is not to be considered legal advice or to be used as a training manual.

From The Author/Publisher

We want to thank you for reading this book! Your interest and desire to obtain knowledge about private investigators and security bear the naked truth about the private sector. They say old investigators do not die. They just fade away with the passing of time as a new investigators carry on.

Hoover's Current Investigative Team / Past Investigators' Names Not Available

Legal process server and former investigator: Pad Finnigan

Investigator associate: Edward Lewis, LPI Service. Mr. Lewis published a book "Hostile Grounds" defusing/restraining violent behavior and physical assaults.

General Investigation Investigator: Janet Harris

Associate professional researcher: Jim Loosen, JAL Data Service, Aberdeen WA. Ex-Washington State Trooper.

Principal/chief investigator: Mel L. Hoover Jr., professional investigator with over 40 years of experience. Agency established 1964 in Tacoma, Wa.

The Hoover Agency has associate contacts in the USA and abroad. Services available just about anywhere in the world.

Dedication

This book is dedicated to the ones we love and that is our family. It is written for the entertainment, history, and knowledge of the private sector with theories and opinions along with informative material on the subject matter covered.

Mel L. Hoover Jr.'s family includes:

Wife Mary O. Hoover, housewife and receptionist for the Hoover agency

Daughter Laurie Ann Hoover, occupation: artist and school teacher, writer of children's books, etc.

Son Monte Hoover, occupation: realtor and window cleaning business owner, and his wife assistant Lauren Hoover, plus home schooling. Children are Christine, Justine, Joshua, and Melissa, who currently is a mother of three children.

Daughter Jennie Kissinger and her husband Dave Kissinger, occupations: Jennie is a nurse, Dave a hospital supervisor. Their children Shandra and David Jr. "DJ."

Son Jerry Hoover and his wife Corinna Hoover, occupations: Jerry works as a concrete technician at Holroyd's and wife runs American Environmental, a meth lab clean-up business. Jerry is also a private pilot. Children are Carlie, Nathan, and Olivia.

Daughter Laurie Wingate and her husband Doug, occupation: tugboat skipper for Crowley Maritime, Laurie is a Technical Assistant 2 with Washington State Energy Program.

Stepson Joe Fredenburg, spouse Iris, Joe's occupation: printer at publishing firm, machine operator.

Hoover, I Spy PI

Table of Contents

Biography: The Makings of a Private Eye

Mel Hoover Jr. was born in 1933 in Tacoma, Washington, a small town in the Great Northwest. People's mode of travel there were vehicles that stemmed from the horse and buggy days. There was crime and suspense in those days too. The making of a PI began when Mel Hoover was born. Call it fate or destiny, the mold began forming a private investigator.

Hoover's background is just one of the ingredients in the making of a private eye. His parents were born in Tacoma too. His father was a general contractor and brick/stone mason. He was law abiding and respected law and order and fair dealings; an honorable man. His spouse, Rose, a devoted housewife and mother, displayed her love for all and understanding ways, loved family, friends and people in general. She loved to cook Italian dinners and entertain the family and friends.

Hoover's grandparents were from Germany. They drifted to Holland and then to the East Coast of America. They moved to Pennsylvania, settling on an island called Hoover Island. The good, bad, and the ugly, as in present times, existed. There were killings in the making among the people, including the Indians. Everyone traded during these times. No money nor jobs existed. Detective work to solve crimes was done by the general community. It is unknown whether a Hoover became a sheriff or not in those days or whether he was just a settler who exchanged commodities with local Indians.

As time went by in the early 1900's, jobs and money became important. Therefore, the settlers pushed westward, fighting the outdoor elements, Indians, and wild animals. There were bandits also who robbed and killed for money along the way. Great-great-grandpapa Hoover moved slowly to the West. His children were born in various states along the way. One son, Montana Hoover, aka Mon, grew up en route to the West coast. He became a young man, fell in love, married a young woman and had children. They moved westwards in various wagon trains. A son and a daughter were born in route on their wagon train adventure. Once again she became pregnant, but the mother and child died and were buried along the train route. The whole family, Mon with his father and mother, moved towards the West.

Hoover's Home Town

City of Tacoma, Washington (Pierce County)

Grandpa & Grandma (Mom / Uncle) Bertocchinni's horse and buggy in the old days on Pacific Ave, Tacoma, Washington

Mon & Hattie Hoover (Grandpa & Grandma)

Mel & Rose Hoover (Mom & Dad) – a mason contractor and housewife

Mon Hoover family

The Hoover bunch

Uncle Clyde Hoover, Army veteran of World War I, became one of 18 state highway patrol officers in the motorcycle division of the Washington State Patrol

Clyde Hoover loved motorcycles. He was one of the first 18 highway patrol officers in Washington's Highway Patrol Motorcycle Division. He rode a Harley Davidson.

Harley Davidson motorcycles have been part of law enforcement for 100 years

State trooper Clyde, after losing his leg and career, became an auxiliary sheriff and a Tacoma city truck driver

Carlo and wife Mary Bertocchinni (Grandpa & Grandma)

Carlo was a Northern Pacific Railway detective and security officer

The family fought the weather and Indians as they went. They arrived in California during the gold rush. Mon Hoover's children were Clyde and Lelia Shasta. Lelia Shasta Hoover, who never married, went to live in Nevada. She wrote and published poety books, and established an alternative health care business (healing with roots, herbs, etc.) at her home. The rest of the family pushed north. Mon Hoover settled in Tacoma. He met Hattie, a widow and a Swede who resided in Stillwater, Minnesota. She came to Tacoma, Washington, by train. Indians and bandits attacked the train en route. They fell in love and were married. Hattie had one son, Glen, from a previous marriage. He was adopted by Mon. The couple had eight children: sons Clyde, Mel (aka Baldy), Woodie, and Glen; and daughters Myrtle, Helen, Lelia, and June. The children grew up with respect and love for their parents, family, and the law. Truth, honesty, and integrity prevailed. All the children grew up, married, and had children of their own in the great Northwest Territory. Lelia married and had two children, Fred and Marilyn. Fred married and has one son, Scott. Woodie, a tanker truck driver, married Emily, they have three children, Little Woodie, Larry and Shelly. Glen married Grace, they have two children, Larry and Lorraine. Myrtle married and has two children, Del and Maxine.

Clyde Hoover went off to the First World War. Afterwards, he returned to Washington, married and divorced, and became one of the first 18 troopers in Washington State. He worked in the motorcycle division, battling crime and making arrests. One day, as his career was growing, he was in high pursuit of a suspected bootlegger. His motorcycle was on the tail of a car while he tried to pull over the suspects. He pulled along side, but the vehicle swung over and hit Clyde's Harley Davidson as they moved fast over the winding country rode. Clyde lost control and he ended up in a road-side ditch. Clyde was knocked unconscious and the motorcycle was on top of him, pinning his mangled and broken leg underneath. After waking up, he was unable to move. Communication was impossible, as this was before two-way radios. He lay there with much pain for hours. There was no vehicle traffic. Finally a car came down the road and discovered Clyde. The occupants took him to the nearest hospital where they discovered the leg was broken and infected. Gangrene had set in. There was no choice but to remove the leg below the knee. Later, an old wooden artificial leg was attached. However Clyde eventually overcame his disability and did everything as he did before losing his leg.

This incident was talked about for many years. However Clyde evaded discussion of the accident. He was disappointed about losing his career with the motorcycle division. But he went on to ride motorcycles again as a Pierce County auxiliary sheriff. He later drove trucks for the

Mel Hoover Jr.'s Rodgers Elementary School in Tacoma, Washington

Mel Hoover Jr. served as a traffic safety patrol officer

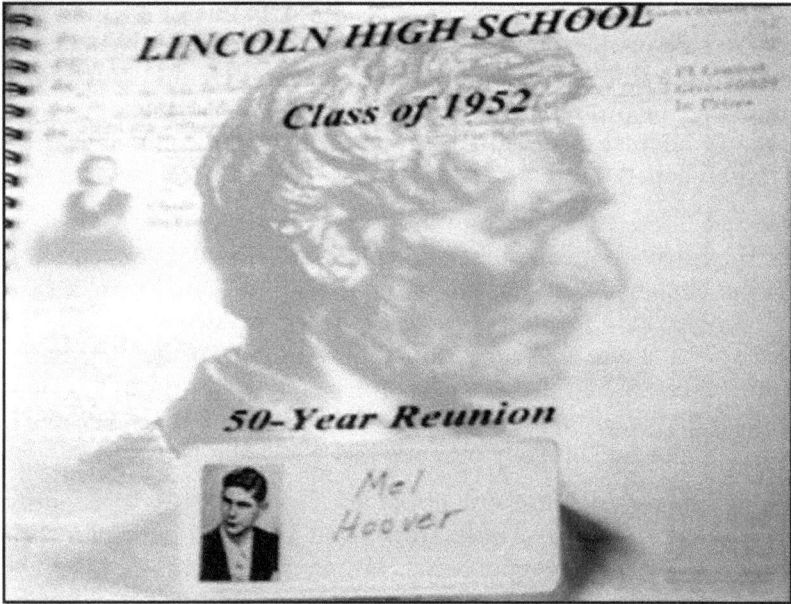

Hoover's Lincoln High School graduation picture at his 50-year reunion

Mel was stationed at Okinawa Air Force Base during the Korean conflict

city of Tacoma and was a member in the local Teamster's Union. He got married, divorced, remarried, and had one son who moved on. He retired to hunt and fish year round on his small farm in Raymond, Washington. The property had a creek running on the back acreage. He had a tame buck deer called Bambie who would come out of the woods when called.

Clyde's dad, Mon Hoover, was really the pioneer of the Teamsters Union. He drove a team of horses and made the first delivery of a flag pole to the Dupont Army Base. His sons Mel and Clyde were part of his delivery team. Clyde had a son, Clyde Jr., known as Peach. He also became a teamster truck driver and ended up with Hoover's trucking business. Mel Jr. was very impressed with the stories they told, especially if they were about law enforcement. Clyde Hoover Jr. got married and had one boy and one girl, Skip and Carlene.

Stories of the past included one about another crime fighting family member, uncle Einar Langseth. He was on Tacoma's police force in the 1940's and became chief of police. He married aunt Helen Hoover and had three children, Al, Jimmie, and Barbara. Al and Jimmie were in the Army Air Force in WW II and flew on the old Flying Fortress, the B-17.

Rose Hoover's family came from Italy. Her father and mother, Carlo and Mary (Petta) Bertocchinni, married in Italy and came to America's East Coast with Mary's brother Frank Petta and her sister. Frank Petta served in the U.S. Navy during World War II. They ended up in Tacoma, where Carlo and Mary had two children, Rosie and Anothony Bertocchinni. Carlo worked for the Northern Pacific Railway on a road gang. Years later he was promoted to a security officer and became an acting railroad detective. His son Tony became head of the Washington State Motor Vehicle Licensing Department, where he remained until forced out at age 70. He belonged to Toastmasters and the Sons of Italy. He made several trips to Italy and met relatives over there (Bertocchinnis). There was a cousin with a family in Tacoma, Washington. Nello and Sara Bertocchinni had one son and two daughters.

Mel Jr.'s dad was a general contractor. He and his helper, Jolly Bowers, borrowed some equipment from an associate contractor. The contractor left his home business and went on a trip. He returned to discover thousands of dollars in cash that he had buried in the back yard missing. The associate contractor accused Mel Hoover Sr. and Jolly Bower of the theft. The county sheriff and his deputies were friends of the contractor. Police brought Hoover Sr. and Jolly Bowers in for questioning. They were given the third degree on the crime and then released.

Hoover's boyhood – learning of the law

Cowboy Mel Hoover Jr. with his parents and horse, Flash

McKinley Hill / Strawberry Hill in Tacoma –
Cowboy Mel Hoover Jr. and his mother and father

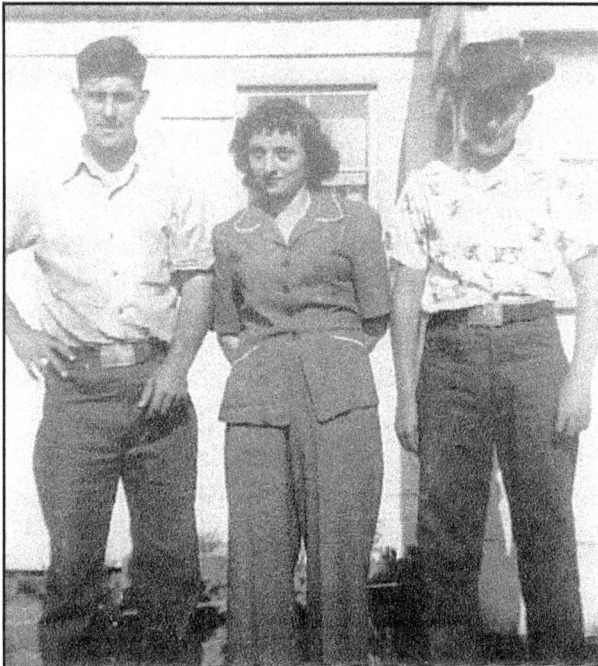

However, bad things began to happen. A couple of Dicks located Jolly Bowers in a tavern one night. They escorted him from the tavern and threw him into a vehicle. He was taken for a ride into the countryside. The dicks questioned him about the cash. Not believing his story, they squeezed his finger tips with pliers in hopes he would reveal where the cash was. They also tried making him talk by using sap gloves, punching him in the face. They were unable to obtain any information from him. They took him home and dropped him off, then quickly left.

Jolly Bowers told Mel Hoover Sr. about the kidnapping, however he made no police report. Bowers' family, wife June and children Dana, Gayle, and Jerry, lived in fear. Jolly also has another son Wayne. Hoover and his wife Rosie and son Mel Jr. were also fearful. Mel Jr., a teenager, secured a weapon to protect his mother while his father worked during the day. Everyone was on their toes as they attempted to put two and two together.

One morning, Mel. Sr. discovered the associate contractor hiding on the premises. He had been eaves dropping. Mel Sr. chased him off the property. He presented evidence to the prosecutor that he and Bowers were innocent of the theft. Mel Sr. told and described the kidnapping of Jolly and the questioning tactics used by the two Dicks and the eaves dropping incident. The prosecutor backed off and the case went away thereafter.

Mel Jr. always had an interest in horses and cars growing up. One Christmas when Mel was a teen, there were no gifts for him under the Christmas tree. Then Mel Sr. suggested that his son look outside. Lo and behold, there as a great surprise to be found: a horse of his own. Mel's eyes almost dropped out of their sockets. As a young teen, he had always played the cowboy part in cowboy clothes. He was known as the neighborhood cowboy and carried the nickname "cowboy." Now with a real horse, the adventures began. He had his own neighborhood cowboy patrol, complete with playing cops and robbers and the detective aspect. He had dreamed of one day being a lawman, a citizen protector, and now his dream came closer to reality.

He received a book during his teens called the G-man. He studied about fingerprinting and made mold castings of footprints and automobile tires. A shy young teen began to grow and develop traits of a lawman, a sheriff, and cowboy detective all rolled into one. In short, he was becoming one good private eye. Subconsciously, he was becoming more sociable, methodic, thinking, and more observant.

Eventually the horses had to go and cars came into the picture during Mel Jr.'s senior year of high school. He got involved with performance cars: a Ford and Mercury hot rods and drag racing. A club was established called the Tacoma Rum Runners. Mel also worked part time as a hod carrier for his father.

Mel. Jr. wondered if his family was relatives of the great FBI Director John Edgar Hoover. There is no evidence of that fact. However, the Hoover family focused on the limelight of Edgar's career. Mel. Jr. also watched movies of Elliot Ness and was an avid follower of the electronic gadgets used by Agent 007.

He graduated from Tacoma's Lincoln High School in 1952. He was summoned to report for military duty because the Korean War was in progress. Mel. Jr. enlisted in the Air Force and so did school mates Danny, Dick, Bud, and Harold. The five were eventually split up. Mel. Jr. trained as a propeller and jet mechanic. He was later stationed at Point Mugu in California and was placed on flight status as the assistant flight engineer in a B-17 drone squadron, the WW II aircraft. Ran missions for the US Navy and Marines. The un-manned B-17 drones were guided by pilots flying in mothership B-17s and the drone aircraft were used as target practice by fighter jets using missiles. Since the missiles they used were without warheads – duds – the drones, when shot, were guided back to the ground. They were then repaired and reused for other missions, including ground to air attacks. Hoover acquired a top-secret security clearance in the 3235th Drone Squadron at the 3205th Naval Air Missile Test Center at Pt. Mugu, California.

Mel received orders to report to a special squadron in Kadena, Okinawa. He was a squadron repair maintenance worker for aircraft props and jet aircraft, assigned to a special detachment that preserved security of the flight line. Special operations worked with CID (Criminal Investigation) including the OSI (Organization of Special Investigations). Worked hand-in-hand with all the branches of the service, Marines, Army, and Air Force, in undercover positions seeking out civilian spies and thefts. Some cases required interpreters. Some civilian Okinawans working for the U.S. Government were spies on the base to do sabotage and espionage.

Mel's special duty in the squadron was to maintain security of the flight line, which included patrol, guard duty, and intelligence gathering duties to prevent sabotage and espionage of the air base. Worked surveillance and interrogations. The north end of the island was communist occupied. Squadrons on base had run bombing

*Late FBI Director
J. Edgar Hoover*

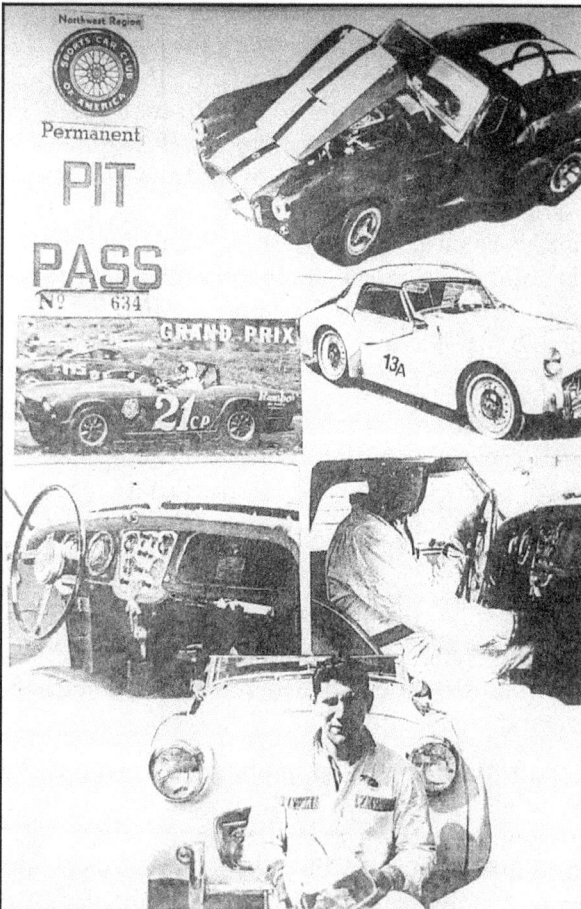

*Mel Hoover Jr.,
novice driver, raced
a 1957 Triumph
TR3 in the Sports
Car Club of
America
(1958–1960)*

*Air Force Sergeant Mel
Hoover Jr. was an
intelligence/security specialist
in F-86 fighter and bomber
squadrons at Kadena Airbase
in Okinawa. A "momason"
carries water in an adjacent
village.*

F-86D jet fighter

Sgt. Mel Hoover writing an intelligence report at his Okinawa desk

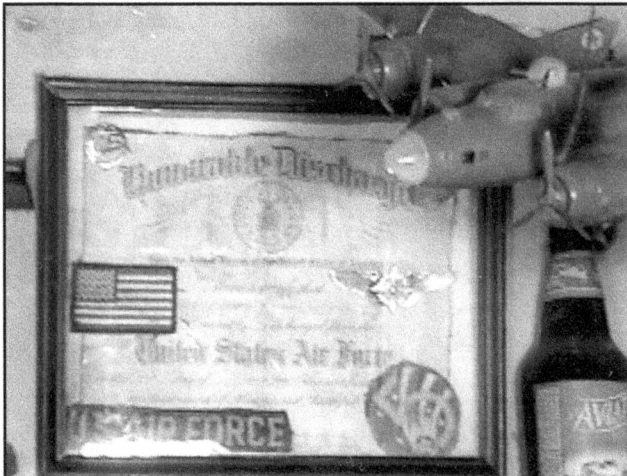

1961 honorable discharge from the Air Force

missions over Korea. US fighter F-86's also engaged Chinese Migs in air-to-air combat near Formosa and the Red China Sea. Squadron salvage crews went to sea to retrieve a downed F-86 in about 500 feet of water. Before the salvage crew arrived, the Chinese had stripped all the machine guns and ammunition from the aircraft, an unbelievable story that was true in every respect. Mel returned to the United States in 1957 and received an honorable discharge in 1961 as a sergeant.

Mel Jr. then was employed by various employers in various jobs. He sought a career in law enforcement. He passed many police department tests, however they could discriminate if people wore glasses or weren't the right height or weight. He therefore was unable to pursue his law enforcement dreams even though he passed many written and physical tests.

When he returned home, he purchased a new TR3 and commenced sport car racing. He raced on most Northwest tracks. Seattle International Raceway was his favorite.

Mel later got married and had three children: Laurie, Monte and Jennie. However domestic problems arose and he divorced. There was a custody battle, and he obtained custody of his children. He remarried and inherited two stepchildren, Joe and Laurie Ann. He and his wife also bore a son, Jerry.

A private detective hired for the custody battle wasn't doing the job, so Mel began his own investigation. He discovered evidence that the children were being neglected and her boyfriend was using the support money to fuel his drinking problem. Then his ex-spouse married and the couple traded the children's home for a ton-and-a-half truck and fled the state with the children, leaving their debts. Mel once again conducted an investigation. He located his ex-spouse's mail drop, tracked down an address, and found them hiding in Twin Falls, Idaho. He hired a private investigator once again. The PI in Twin Falls who did a good job investigating and noting the conditions they were living in. Therefore, evidence presented to the judge resulted in custody of the children being awarded to Mel. The kicker was trading off the children's home for the ton-and-a-half truck. The ex-spouse was later divorced again for about the fourth time.

The blended Hoover family had grown to include three boys, Joe, Monte, and Jerry, and three girls, Laurie, Jennie, and Laurie Ann. Hoover Jr. maintained a job and began working part time with various detective agencies. He received hands-on job experience working on cases. He also took private investigation and law enforcement courses.

The Tacoma Police Department provided special Polic Commissions to private investigators. Mel received a commission Dec. 17, 1964. The Hoover Investigation Agency was established from that day on to the present.

Mel maintained membership in local, state, and international private investigators associations in order to have contacts worldwide. Hoover specialized in all phases of investigations, leaving no pages unturned. In 1982 he was vice president for the Law Enforcement Association. He also maintained membership with the World Association of Detectives and the Pacific Northwest Association of Investigators.

Mel stated, "Being all you can be is success. It stems from an inner drive and enjoying what you do. Doing your best and pushing it to the limit. The investigator's theory is "never leave a stone unturned." Be a professional. Professionalism is the key to success, too."

The making of a private eye are the qualities described within this book. Plus it is important to have a good family background, morals in which you know right from wrong, and to be able to think clearly. To prove or disprove your case, you have to figure out the puzzle with known facts. Respect and devotion to the profession requires accuracy in fact finding, producing the truth with honesty, and holding yourself up with integrity. Accurate reports need facts that are solid as a rock. Reports must be produced with precision in every detail with no holes. They must show all the facts and details in the case in a strict manner, supported by evidence that's true to form.

For a professional private investigator in the private-sector, character is a plus. It comes from your background, your roots. You must be honest, truthful, fair dealing, respectful, tolerant, patient, understanding, and have integrity. Sometimes a person's occupation can be a natural thing without much training and he can be very successful without much effort. In making of a private eye, or any other occupation, it's a matter of finding yourself in life and establishing your goals and all your priorities. In this book known as "Hoover, I Spy PI (namely one I-Spy character, Mel Hoover Jr.), a small detective agency is classified as being successful in its own way for being around over 40 years.

There are more than 65,000 private investigators and more than 26,000 agencies in the United States. Each agency employs on the average 2.5 investigators. Investigators' salaries before taxes range from approximately $20,000 to $75,000 per year. Agencies range from $75,000 to about $125,000+ per year. You cannot determine the investigator's or the agency's success by their income alone.

Seminar by William C, Dear, International Private Detective for Private Investigators.

Photo obtained by Edward Lewis of LPI Services.

The seminar featured:

- –Murder Cases, Solved and Unsolved
- –Murder or Suicide?
- –Field Endeavors and Lack of Cooperation
- –Who, What, When,Where, Why
- –Never Assume and Always Verify What's in a Crime Scene
- –Photograph Scene, Examie Crime Scene
- –Obtain Witnesses
- –Stumbling Blocks for the Private Investigator
- –Useful Ways to Work with the Police
- –Utilizing the Press and Media
- –Treat Investigations as if Crime Has Just Been Found, Even Though Being Investigated by the Police
- –Rewards are Emotional and Financial

Seminar introduction photo – Hoover, Rice, Harris, Dear, and the Lewis Brothers

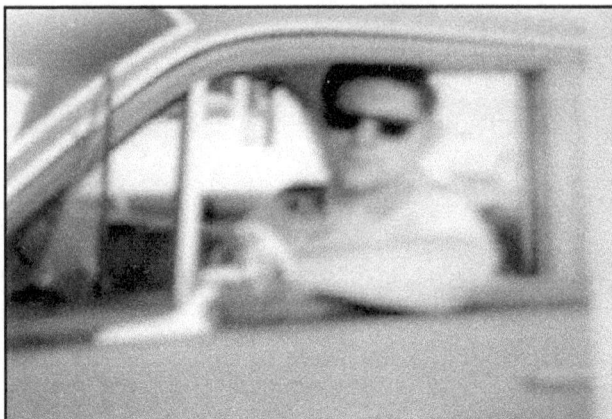

Vehicle contact

INVESTIGATOR
City of Tacoma
SPECIAL
POLICE OFFICER

| DATE ISSUED | EXPIRATION |
| 12-17-65 | Indefinite |

SPECIAL IDENTIFICATION

DATE OF BIRTH

NAME Melvin L. Hoover, Jr. 5-14-3

5'11"
180 lbs.
COLOR HAIR Brown
COLOR EYES Hazel

Badge No. **1643**

Identification

Identifying himself during a drug apprehension

Mel Hoover Jr.'s children
alongside a sheriff's search
and rescue unit

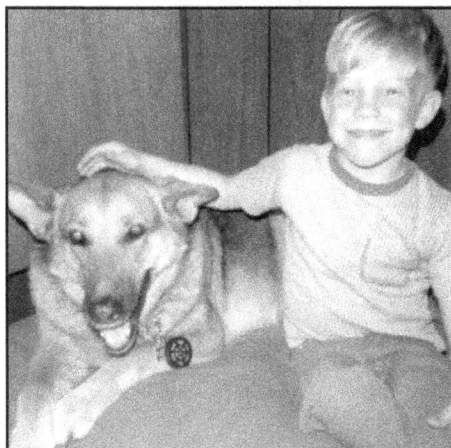

Youngest son Jerry with German
Sheppard guard dog, "Shatzy"

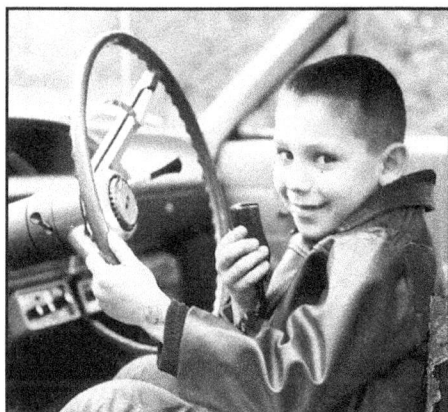

Oldest son Monte, named after
great-grandpa Montana Hoover,
working Dad's 2-way radio in
the private investigator's vehicle

In later years, investigator Hoover was a supporter of motocross racing

Son Jerry raced on the motocross circuit for several years and won many trophies, usually taking third place

Seen in his third place position – lucky number 3s

World recognition is surely a success story in itself. However, for US private eyes who do not receive any recognition, it doesn't mean they are not successful private investigators.

Note that most professional investigators in present day are truly professionals with updated training in city, state, and federal laws. They attend seminars to keep them current. The Legislature also has required them to be licensed and bonded and insured. The Hoover investigators depicted in this book are surely professionals and do not portray TV detectives. Many investigators specialize and some generalize by handling all phases of investigations, as does Hoover Investigations.

Private investigators' characteristics, as discussed in this book, include good common sense, sociable, able to get along with people in general, conversational, and truth seeking. Being sociable is a key tool in obtaining the cooperation of others.

Hoover and the agency have used these traits year after year. In addition to being sociable, it is advisable to first check people's backgrounds, if possible. Always have a sense of humor and know a person's favorite topic. It is also beneficial to be kind, cordial, courteous, and to add some charm.

Having contacts in your local area is a must in gathering information. Once confidence has been established with your contacts, many people will be willing to open their lips and their hearts and souls, spilling out their guts to you. These contacts will be there if and when you need them. When the time arises, you will be able to obtain the information you need.

Biography: The Makings of a Private-Eye, Conclusion

Being a successful investigator in private investigations requires good old common sense and wits. As previously mentioned, being sociable is a very good trait for successfully gaining and maintaining the cooperation of others and obtaining the information you may need. Also, a sense of good humor, kindness, cordiality, and charm also work to the advantage of the private investigator.

A private investigator should have many local contacts and sources of information (a smile costs nothing and buys everything), including:

people in all walks of life (street people)	taxi cab drivers
bankers	business persons
associations	news reporters
bartenders and waitresses	scholars

They all can provide information and documents to support a case assignment. Good information solves cases. Computers and high technology will never replace the mind of man, no matter what happens.

There will always be a need for a good, professional private-eye.

Private eye Mel Hoover maintained surveillance on a private residence from his van.

Undercover Investigation

The Hoover Agency was contacted by a corporate officer who set a meeting with Mel Hoover Jr., chief investigator. The company was loosing large amounts of cash, possibly $100,000 per day. The meeting took place away from the corporate office in a quiet, secured restaurant. The case was discussed at length, and all the pertinent information was obtained. The trucking company transported high tech computer equipment and chips. At the end of the lunch meeting, the customer paid a retainer to Hoover to investigate the losses.

It appeared to be an internal problem with the company's truck drivers. Chief investigator Hoover picked two of his best agents to be placed inside the company. That was ideal because the company had run a newspaper advertisement for employment positions. Undercover work can determine what is going on inside the company. Only one corporate officer knew what was going on and maintained contact with chief Mel Hoover Jr. The undercover agents' only contact was with the chief.

A background investigation was begun on all suspects within the company. The undercover agents remained discrete once placed in the company. After the company hired 10 employees, even the contact corporate officer was unaware of the agents' identities. The operation had to remain discrete at all costs. There could always be a possible leak, which had to be prevented at all costs. People can become paranoid, especially if they are doing something wrong. Undercover operations have to be kept discrete or the operation could be blown and undercover agents could be put at risk. The corporation had security agents. But the security director did not know of the internal investigation, only the corporate officer knew.

Hoover's agents settled into the company, learning about the employees and the company's procedures in transporting the equipment. With time, patience, and observation, intelligence was gathered.

The agents zoomed in on two suspects. They were truck drivers who transported the goods. Equipment crates were inspected, but agents noticed that the yellow shipment manifests had been altered to divert the merchandize elsewhere without a trace. Agents placed micro-transmitters on several of the cases being delivered by the suspected drivers. Agents synchronized their receivers to the transmitters. The trucks left the warehouse and it was discovered that both trucks were traveling the same route.

Agents took off after the trucks, keeping some distance behind the trucks as they drove through city streets and then onto the freeway northbound at a pretty good rate of speed. Agents had their small, discrete receivers in their vehicles. Agents kept out of sight of the trucks, using the receiving signal to keep up with them.

The trucks exited the freeway onto a county road in a heavily wooded area at the base of the Cascade Mountains. Agents tracked them, staying out of sight. They noticed that the trucks went on a private road in a very secluded wooded area surrounded by brush and high fir trees.

The agents knew the trucks had stopped in the area as confirmed by the transmitters' receiving signal. The merchandise packages were stationary.

Agents hid their vehicles and both went on foot with two-way hand-held transceivers. The agents split up, going on each side of the private road and keeping out of sight. They worked their way up to the road. Approximately half a mile in the distance they spotted an old warehouse. The garage doors were open, and they noted the trucks were backed up side-by-side at the garage door opening.

The agents, using their two-way radios, decided to work their way around to the rear of the garage. They encountered a dog in doing so. The dog barked and alerted the men inside. They came out and looked around. The agents had taken cover in the brush. The dog was quieted down by the truck drivers. Later, a dog moved towards the agents, its hair standing straight up. However, it wasn't barking, only moving on the prowl and seeking out its prey. It so happened that one of the agents was carrying a dart gun. A dart would tranquilize a storming bull to sleep. The dog approached. It was a large Pit Bull showing his teeth with his hair standing on end. He started barking again, ready to attack the agents. The agent fired the dart gun, hitting the Pit Bull in the neck and putting it instantly to sleep.

Agents were finally on each side in the rear of the warehouse building. They were able to work their way to windows looking into the garage. They observed that the rear ends of the trucks were open and that the men were unloading the cases in question. Agent Frank reached into his pocket and removed a small digital video camera. He zoomed in on the men unloading the merchandise. The video said it all: the time, date, location, company trucks with their Washington plate numbers and the company name on the side, the warehouse, and identified the men and their activities.

The agents worked their way back to their hidden vehicles and bee lined out of the immediate area. They situated themselves out of sight and observed the private road. Agent Frank, in charged, reached for his cell phone and called chief investigator Hoover. Hoover in turn called the corporate officer. Both called the local police. As luck would have it, there was a patrol unit in the immediate area. The police arrived on the scene and made contact with the agents. They then zoomed in on the trucks and arrested the drivers. Charges were filed for thefts that occurred within the company.

The men went to trial, were convicted and sentenced to prison.

GPS Unit

Antenna

Weatherproof Cover

PROTRAK Scout
Low-cost GPS Data Logger

Software

YOUR VEHICLE IS HERE

Court Room
Private Investigator's Testimony

Case #1

Investigator Mel Hoover was called upon to investigate a possible fraud situation. A common name was given and the subjects in question had no available address in the attorney's file. Hoover's agency personnel began a computer search on the subjects in question. No information was obtained on the male subject. However, they did locate their place of business. Another computer search on the businesses revealed the male and female subjects were somehow tied together.

An investigator used a pretext to go to a bookstore to learn about mail drop boxes setup inside for special mail services. The investigator learned the two subjects' names. They owned several book stores plus a newly opened restaurant.

The following day, the investigator went to the restaurant with a hidden camera. He observed and video taped the female subject and learned her identity. The video showed her working and her teenage daughter. Later, the male subject arrived. He determined the two were in fact married to one another. Their two identical Mercedes Benz sedans sat outside. During the evening shift, the male remained at the restaurant while the mother and daughter departed in one Mercedes. They drove to a residential area in University Place and pulled into a parking pad in front of a double garage door. The car pulled inside and the door closed. Investigator Hoover filmed the events.

Hoover returned to the agency office and researched more records. He later obtained documents showing the male and female subjects had been married in a foreign country and had two teenage children, a boy and a girl. The male subject's name was used as owning the vehicles and businesses. The female subject's name was not provided. The male, upon entering the United States, changed his name to the common American name, Johnson. The female was his lawful spouse and the children were their biological children. The female and the two children were drawing welfare from the Department of Health Services. But she was a working partner in the businesses and lived with her husband and children in a $300,000 home.

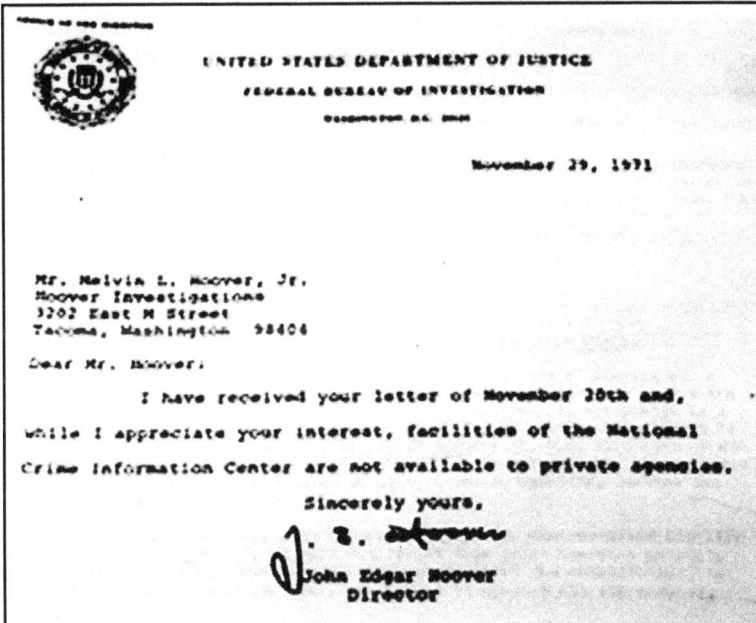

Hoover Agency correspondence with FBI Director J. Edgar Hoover

A reply from the acting FBI director after Hoover sent a sympathy letter following J. Edgar Hoover's sudden death

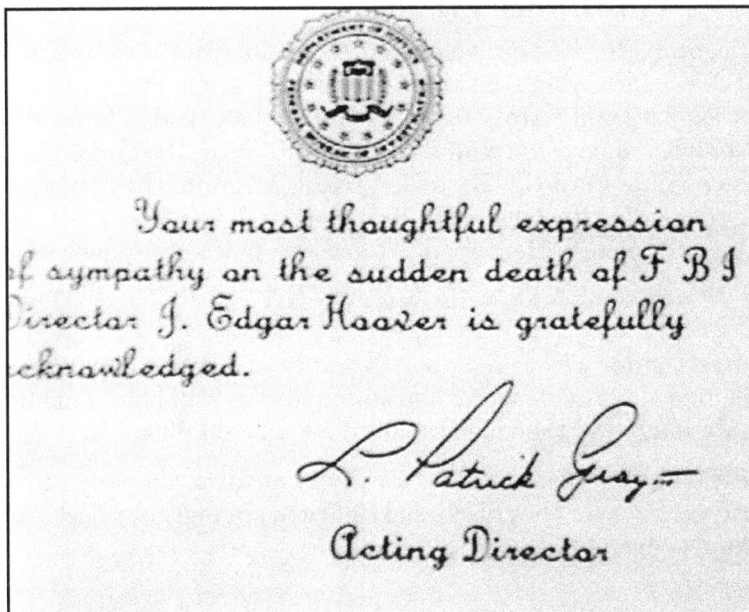

Hoover submitted his report to the law firm and the attorney handling the case. Action was taken, and charges were brought against the two for welfare fraud. A trial was scheduled and the investigator was summoned to testify.

The investigator reported to the court room in a suit and tie to provide testimony. The investigator was placed on the stand and sworn in to tell the truth, the whole truth. He gave direct testimony on documents obtained about the female and on the video evidence. Testimony was given in a well mannered, polite tone. He didn't understand several questions and had the attorney repeat them before answering.

The investigator followed guidelines for good testimony during cross examination by the opposing attorney for the female subject. Remember, when telling the truth, everyone is looking for the truth. However it's the job of the defense attorney to win the case.

The investigator's testimony showed that he took the video of the persons, objects, and scenes as a general photographer, not an expert professional photographer.

The female subject was found guilty of fraud by the jury. The judges ordered a specified amount of jail time and a specific amount to be repaid to DHS.

Case #2 – Insurance Fraud

Investigator Mel Hoover was hired by an insurance company on a fraud case concerning a disabled man who was claiming a bad back and a leg he could hardly move. Hoover set up surveillance on the man for a few days. One sunny day, the subject walked briskly out to his convertible Ford GT. He took a flying leap into the driver's seat without opening the door. He drove off and went to a residence, parking at the curb. He leaped out and ran to the front door. Hoover took still and video pictures to document the man's identity and actions.

The investigator was called upon to testify in a deposition regarding the photographic evidence he had obtained. The still photos identified the individual and the videos showed he was not disabled.

The investigator was contacted by the insurance company attorney regarding the case. They discussed Hoover's photography background and knowledge.

Hoover testified that he was qualified in general photography and that the photography was original and was taken by himself. He said it was unaltered, accurate, and represented the action at the scene at the time of the surveillance.

The investigator's objective was to seek the truth and to assist the court, a vital role contributing to the due process of the law.

While on the stand, the investigator gave his testimony and then the opposing attorney began cross examination. The attorney attempted tactics to relax the investigator, trying to gain his confidence. He attempted to lead the witness into saying something he didn't mean. He was unsuccessful. If he had succeeded, he would quickly have gone for the throat by discrediting the testimony and possibly alleging perjury. The attorney also attempted trick questions, asking for yes or no answers, but the investigator didn't fall for his trap. He remained natural and polite. He used no slang terms and did not give positive answers when he was in doubt about how to answer a question. He always addressed the judge as "your honor" and then answered the question. During recess, several people approached Hoover to try to talk to him about the case. It appeared to be a set up deal by the defense. It didn't work!

After the recess, Hoover got back on the stand and cross examination by the defense attorney resumed. He shifted his questioning and asked, "Who told you how to testify?" Hoover answered loudly that no one had instructed him on how to testify.

If the investigator made a mistake, he corrected himself without any hesitation. He maintained good facial expressions and never got out of line. He let the defense attorney expose himself. Hoover volunteered no information. He maintained professionalism. As questioning continued regarding the video, Hoover said that he was the photographer and that the video was unaltered. He was asked if he were a professional photographer. Hoover answered, "No." He specified that he is not an expert with knowledge about everything in the field, such as the physics of light and optics. He said he was qualified as a general photographer and that the film was original, unaltered, accurate, and represents the scene at the time of the surveillance.

The case photographs and testimony submitted by Hoover were enough evidence against the claimant that his attorney settled the matter outside of Superior Court.

There are seven guidelines the investigator follows while serving justice, telling the truth, and being honest:

1. Listen carefully to questions, and pause before answering. Think, and be sure to understand the question completely.

2. Answer truthfully. Use terms such as, "That's all I remember," or "I don't know," or "It's to the best of my knowledge."

3. Answer simply, using yes or no when possible. Never elaborate unless clarifications are necessary. Never volunteer information.

4. Give direct answers. Do not exaggerate answers. Make them short and think them through well before answering

5. Avoid allowing the opposing attorney place words in your mouth. Be alert and watch for trick questions, such as wording the same question differently or asking for comparisons or analogies.

6. Be calm and cool. Don't be sarcastic, argumentative, combative, or a wise guy. Don't become rattled or intimidated by questioning.

7. Don't display emotions such as anger, fatigue, or impatience. Testify slowly with the truth and well thought out answers to questions. Testifying in a calm and convincing manner is the mark of a professional.

Photo taken August 2000

Pierce County Superior Court Judges

Unsolved Murders of Document Examiners

Investigator Mel Hoover would contact document examiners who were his associates and friends to perform document service assignments. He met one man and wife team through the Pacific Northwest Association of Investigators in about 1968. They were locally and internationally known. On murder and theft cases, the male examiner would lift latent fingerprints and palm prints from many objects at crime scenes. On fraud cases, he'd examine documents for any and all alterations, including the seals and handwriting, to prove or disprove forgery.

The male examiner had good resources for comparing latent prints. He used AFIS, Automated Fingerprint Individual Print Scan, which detects matches to individuals at the rate of 500 per second with great accuracy. Law enforcement uses NCIC, the National Crime Information Center. It checks nationwide for criminal information for photos on subjects based on latent fingerprints and palm prints. Its crime lab produces information on warrants, stolen property, and missing persons. There are about 17,000 computer terminals nationwide, and the system is growing very rapidly.

The document examiner was a forensic specialist. He examined for Hoover on theft and murder cases. He lifted prints, made foot and tire casing molds, and analyzed patterns in weapons, bullets, cartridges, or powder. He did assignments by the case. The man-wife team worked for the State of Washington as fraud investigators, for the Department of Social and Health Services (welfare), and provided services for attorneys and private eyes.

The wife had a masters degree from the International Graphoanalysis Society and was classified as an expert in handwriting analysis. Her husband worked for 25 years for the Seattle Police Department, 15 years of it in the crime lab.

He and his wife helped solve many cases for attorneys, private eyes, and, of course, for prosecutors of welfare fraud cases in Washington's Department of Social and Health Services.

The couple resided in the West side of Seattle in a fairly modest, nice home in a nice neighborhood. Both were noted to be the best in their profession. Investigators, attorneys, and private eyes who knew and dealt with the couple said, "You couldn't have known a better, friendly,

Seattle, Washington, where two document examiners were murdered

The male and female document examiner victims in the unsolved murder

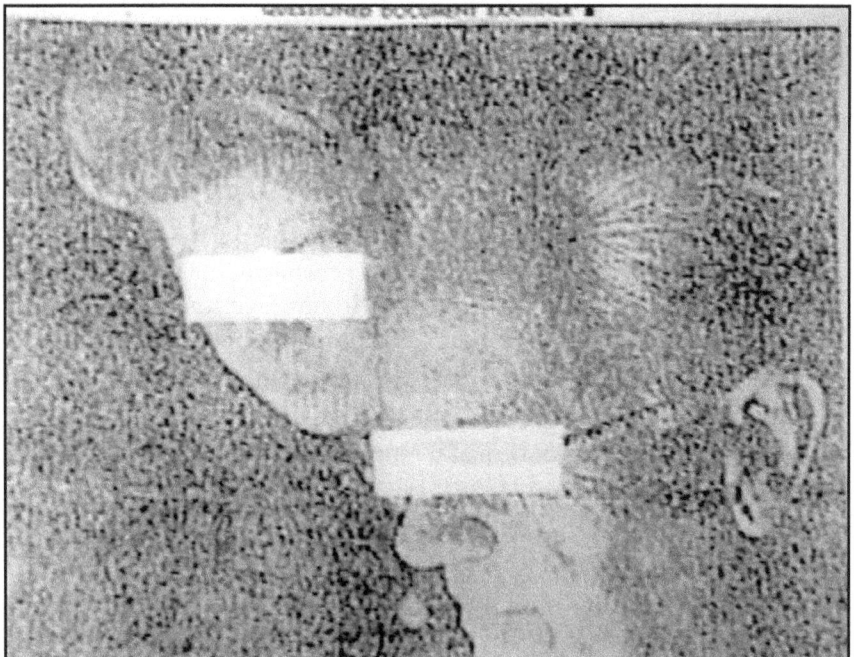

loveable, nicer couple to work with." They lived in their home for 40 years. It had a fenced back yard with a lawn. They had a large German Shepherd they called "Tippy." The dog was trained to be a good watchdog and would let you know if anyone was about the premises. They posted a "Beware of the Dog" sign.

They conducted business out of their home. They used the main floor living room area for conferences. They obtained some of their assignments from PIs and attorneys, and maintained contacts with other state officials by telephone, etc. In their basement was a very up-to-date laboratory with various types of high-tech equipment for examining documents and a darkroom.

In the document examiners' basement was work space to use their knowledge and experience to expose cheats and frauds. They also had other crime-related equipment, forms, and paper work to compare fingerprints, firearm ballistics tests, and bullet comparisons.

Investigator Hoover used their services on various cases from time to time. He became friends with the two. They enlightened him on many cases and helped convict frauds and murderers in large numbers. Hoover and the couple conversed on a large variety of cases. One day, they talked about threats. Hoover mentioned threatening phone calls he had received through the years. They talked openly about the telephone threats. The couple stated they were not concerned at all about the threats they received through the years. The investigator confirmed that he also had paid no mind to the threatening telephone calls he had received through the years. The couple always appeared calm and cool, as was Hoover, and took everything with a grain of salt. They said, "I never, never spent any time at all wasting time thinking about those telephone threats."

Years later, the threats became a reality. In the mid-1980's, the couple's only son made a very gruesome discovery when he came home to the residence and found that his parents had been attacked and murdered. There was no sign of a struggle. He made a report to the Seattle Police Department. An investigation of the murder's suspicious circumstances took place. Police examined the scene and checked for fingerprints and forensic evidence. It was classified as a double homicide. The dog "Tippy" was in the basement alive and well. The entire house was ransacked.

The Seattle police detectives began a massive homicide investigation. Mel Hoover and other private investigators volunteered time to help investigate this terrible double homicide event. They all put their

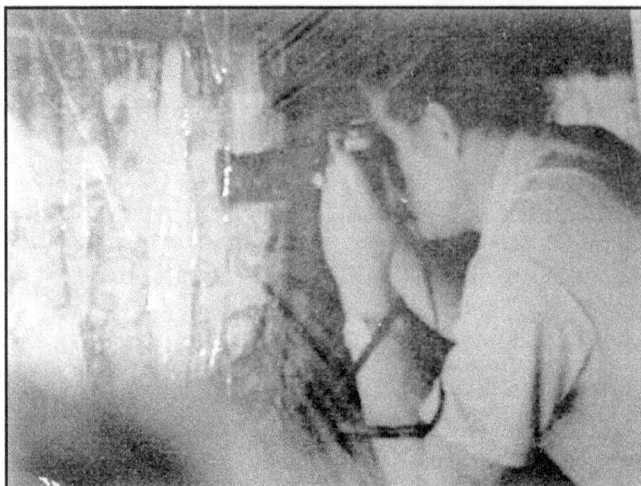

Hoover shooting 35mm photographs from a covert van during a stakeout

An ID badge and weapon are tools of the trade

The Hoover Agency office in Tacoma, Washington. There will always be a need for a good investigator.

heads together in an attempt to bring justice and closure to this crime. They looked into the modus operandi (MO); was it revenge, theft, or a random killing? Hoover developed a theory that the person or persons who entered the house had to have been known to the couple and were greeted with open arms or were taken off guard at the door. Their German Sheppard, "Tippy," apparently knew the subject or subjects. There was no sign of a struggle, no force entry, no sign of armed robbery, and no valuable merchandize or furnishing had been removed from the home. Everything appeared in tact inside the home. Hoover believed the dog was removed from the upstairs floor and was placed in the basement by someone who knew them and their dog. However, the house had been ransacked upstairs. Dresser drawers were opened and the clothes closet had been gone through. Nothing had been taken.

Past and present criminal case records were scanned for suspects. They also looked for friends or neighbors who had close relations or contact with the couple and who had a criminal record or who had been convicted by the couple. The son had been working out of town at the time of the homicides. The couple had no other relatives.

Law enforcement personnel and private eyes came to a dead end, unable to obtain any physical evidence or suspects or leads on the case. The case remains an open book.

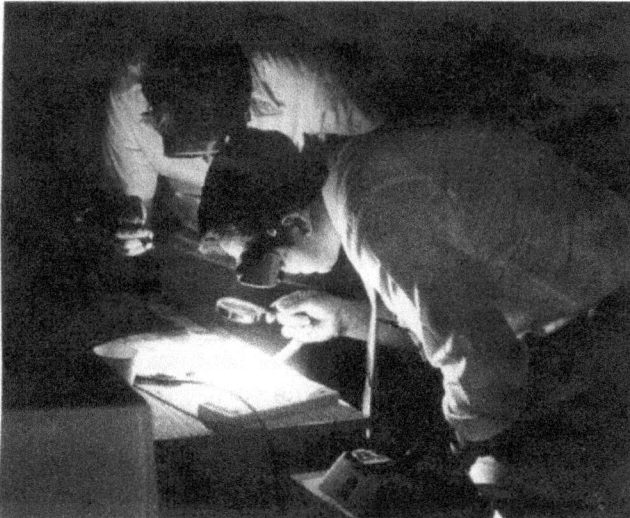

Laser illumination of latent prints

Medical Malpractice Case

The Hoover Agency was contacted by an attorney representing a medical doctor. He spoke with Mel Hoover, chief investigator. He said the doctor had treated a middle-aged patient, and the patient initiated a lawsuit against the doctor claiming he was fully disabled and could no longer to work at his place of business. He claimed his condition worsened after the doctor's treatment.

Hoover arranged with the attorney to run surveillance on the patient. It started at the patient's residence and at the adjacent large nursery the patient owned and ran.

The surveillance continued day by day and Hoover used patience through the course of the week. On three different occasions, the male patient was observed moving from his home to the nursery and working with flowers and shrubbery there.

The surveillance was performed from a wooded area across from the residence and nursery. It was dull and unrewarding at times. Hoover remained very patient during the week, observing and filming the patient's activities from a wooded area. The investigator blended into the woods, out of sight. He identified the subject by his physical description, his residence, and the vehicles outside the residence. An investigator keeps an open mind and notices what is going on in the environment surrounding him. One needs to be in good physical shape to move about and be able to respond quickly to document activities. A written report and video documents the location, date, time and place.

Hoover video taped the subject doing work, walking and moving swiftly about his home and the business. He attended to customers on a daily basis. On the last day, Hoover taped the best of the subject's activities. The subject left his home and walked to the nursery. He attended to some customers who walked about the nursery for over 30 minutes. They decided to purchase a large tree. The customer moved his truck as close as he could to the tree. The subject then wrestled the tree into the truck bed, bending at the knees, stretching, reaching, dragging, and lifting the tree into the truck. He displayed no visible sign of pain or strain, but did show he was capable of getting the tree into the truck. The customers left with the tree in their truck.

Hoover later observed the subject carrying a large ladder and placing against the side of the nursery building. He obtained a can of paint and a brush and began painting the trim on the building. He moved the ladder from time to time, and climbed up and down the ladder constantly as he painted the trim. Hoover video taped the activity. He displayed no pain or strain regarding his back or legs or arms. His body movement appeared to be in tip top shape.

At a deposition in the lawsuit, the tape was viewed by the opposing attorney. He settled the case out of court. The viewing of Hoover's tape effectively closed the case.

A Worker's Compensation Surveillance

Investigator Hoover was summoned by a company to perform surveillance on a male employee who was collecting disability benefits from the company. Because it was costing them money, an attorney representing the company's insurance policy discussed the case with Mel Hoover. Arrangements were made to watch the subject for one week.

He had injured his back at work and claimed to be in great pain. He said it was hard to walk, stand, or lay down, and therefore he was unable to work. A doctor had treated his back for almost a year.

Hoover initiated surveillance from a van he set up in the community. It blended in with surrounding vehicles in the area. The van had a roof vent that housed a video lens that could scan 360 degrees around the van. The lens was set up with a periscope system, allowing the operator to see the person and his activities through the scope or on a color TV monitor equipped with a VCR for recording. The lens had zoom capabilities to zoom up close on the male subject. Inside the van, a large swivel chair faced the periscope and monitor. Hoover also used a cell phone and a two-way radio to maintain contact with his office.

During the winter, surveillance from the van can get awfully cold. In the summer it becomes extremely hot. So the clothing worn is important. Some vans, however, are equipped with a heating and cooling system. A good porta-potti comes in handy, too, along with a cooler and a sandwich or two.

Days went by with no activities by the subject noted. A good eagle eye is necessary to find a subject. The investigator must be alert, ready, and willing to play out his hunches, gut, or feelings on the matter. As one sits and waits, tension builds up. So you must try to relax and be as comfortable as possible, stretching and flexing your muscles as you utilize your mind to concentrate on the target.

A male subject who fit the employee's description was finally observed. A close up photo taken of the man was identified as the target subject. Hoover later video taped him walking and even running to visit his doctor. Information had been given to Hoover that the subject did visit his doctor on a regular basis.

The investigator, following a hunch and gut feeling, set up surveillance during an evening period. On that evening, the subject happened to leave his residence in his vehicle. Hoover followed him to a company that made overhead garage doors. The man parked his vehicle and went in. It was the start of a swing shift, and Hoover saw the man through the window working at a table jigging door panels for the company. He took video photos of those activities. Further investigation determined that the man was being paid under the table for his work there.

The employee was deposed by the employer's insurance company attorney. Once the man saw the video of his activities, he confessed that he was defrauding the company. The case was closed.

NIGHT VISION

IR ILLUMINATORS & LONG RANGE LENSES

THERMAL IMAGING

IR MAXA BEAM

VIDEO RELAY LENS

VIDEO INTERFACE

Domestic Case – Child Custody

A Viet Nam veteran was married for a number of years, and during his wartime tour in Viet Nam, he was shot trying to save some villagers. He was partially disabled and was discharged from the service when he returned to the United States.

Along with his honorable discharge and disability pay, he began to support himself in business. He needed the business as therapy to recover from his war experience and to provide better things for his family.

He had some problems in his marriage, and he found that his wife had worked in a strip joint without his knowledge. He also learned she had been doing drugs – pot. They separated and then divorced. During the court proceedings, he attempted to gain custody of his boy and girl. He lost the custody case. He did gain visitation rights with his children and paid child support.

A year later he remarried a woman with two children. At the time his children had grown and were 9 and 10 years old. His former wife was very secretive about her activities, but during visitations, the children told their father that their mom had allowed them to come to bed with her while she had another man in bed with her. They told their father this man touched them in their private parts while he was on top of their mother in bed.

The father had heard enough of this, so he went to his attorney and explained what the children had told him on numerous visitations with him. They contacted a child psychiatrist to begin sessions with the children during their visitations with the father. During those sessions, the children spoke in detail about the information they had told their father, indicating that the stories they had told their father were apparently true.

The father's attorney advised the disabled veteran that an investigation was needed to prove what was happening to the children. The man contacted investigator Mel Hoover who listened to the man's story. An investigation contract was signed to begin the investigation.

Hoover began surveillance on the mother's residence. It was a two-story, old, run-down house with exposed windows around the dwelling. The house was in unkempt condition inside and out. Hoover noted that a 1970 4-door Ford parked outside an adjacent house belonged to the mother's boyfriend. It was a dark blue sedan with Washington license plates.

The investigator ran a background check on the license plates and learned the name of the male subject and his last known address. Computer and physical record searches confirmed the subject's name and his physical description. That information matched court record information establishing his date of birth, address, physical description and his history. He had a long rap sheet indicating he had been involved in contributing to prostitution, selling and possessing drugs, burglary, and theft.

Continuing surveillance confirmed that the man was residing in the house with the children. When the two adults left the house, they left the children with a teenage babysitter. Hoover determined that the mother worked evenings at a local topless place. He also video taped the man selling drugs in the parking lot after he had transported her to her workplace.

The children's mother worked the floor inside the topless establishment. Hoover observed her inside and noted she was very pleasant with her customers. Her figure was outstanding, just like a model or a movie star. She was full busted and apparently had breast implants because she was a good 48 size. Her buttocks were well proportioned for her figure. She had long legs and very long blonde hair that streamed down her bare backside. The customers were in awe of her, and their eyes were glued on her in amazement. Hoover placed a covert pinhole camera and VCR on himself and acquired video tape of her beautiful moves.

The mother was a topless go-go dancer. Hoover video taped her when her song played and she began to strip. Her boyfriend came in and sat adjacent to the stage drinking a beer. On stage, her movements were breathless. She exposed herself as she peeled off her high heel shoes and then her bra. Everyone's eyes were glued to her. Everyone roared and clapped while her body twisted and her large breasts bounced up and down. The investigator obtained it all on the discretely hidden camera and miniature VCR. She bore the naked truth.

After her dance routine ended, she hit the crowd for table dances. Everyone wanted one, paying out many dollars to her. Hoover left the establishment.

The next evening, surveillance resumed at her residence. The investigator located himself discretely and out of sight of surrounding neighbors. He blended into the environment. This was her night off from work at the strip joint. Hoover's gut feeling was that it was possible the couple would remain at the house. Through the open windows, he observed them inside with the children, moving from room to room. Later, the curtains closed on the lower floor and the lights were extinguished at 10 pm. The lights then came on in the upper main room of the house. The curtains were half way open so Hoover had visibility of the top half of a large bed that could just barely be seen. It was a lucky break. The children came into the room with their mother and began bouncing on the bed as the mother disrobed and stood naked, showing her beautiful body. Her boyfriend then popped in through the door completely naked. He grabbed the mother, embraced her, and began kissing her breast. He worked down between her legs. Hoover used a telephoto lens on a video camera and tripod to film every single event. He also used a long telephoto 35 mm still camera with high speed film. The couple fell onto the bed where the children were laying.

Hoover presented his client and the attorney with his report with supporting video evidence. They had a Superior Court case on the docket. On the day of court, the investigator met with the client and his attorney at the court house prior to an appearance in front of the judge.

Everyone rose as the judge entered the courtroom to begin the court session. However, the client's ex-wife did not show up and neither did her attorney. The judge reviewed the still photos of the mother and her boyfriend and the children in the bedroom scene.

The father was awarded custody of his minor children.

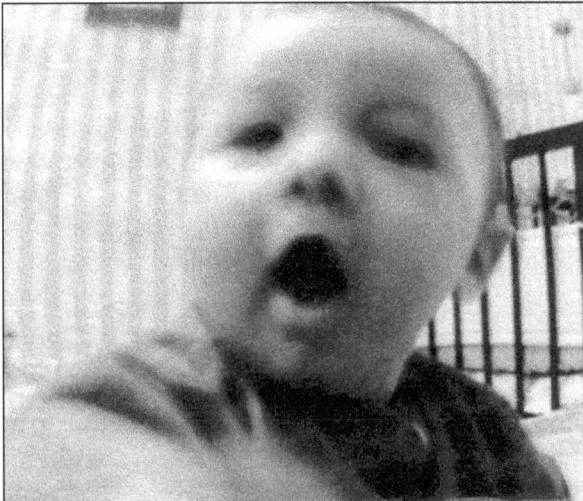

Hidden pin-hole camera, watching a child

Domestic Information – Child Custody

In domestic cases, child custody is usually the basic issue. The welfare of the minor children is the primary consideration. There are relevant factors to be considered by the investigator to prove or disprove the case.

Upon receiving all the facts through investigation, the investigator presents them to the client and their attorney. They may also be included in the guardian ad litem's investigation report. The combined reports are the determining factors used to judge what custody arrangement is in the best interest of the minor children. The Superior Court judge analyzes the evidence presented and makes the final decision about where custody will be placed.

Factors that are considered include sex and age of the children, their inter-reactions with the parents, their custody wishes and those of the parents, and possible changes to the child's home, school, and community. Also considered are the mental and physical health of the children and parents. The parents' financial status, stability, religious status and sexual and moral background are also factors. Race and ethnic background of the parents and children are also considered. The parents' relationships with the children, their acceptance of one another, their daily interaction, the consistency of hands-on care such as discipline and over-all supervision are important. The children's educational opportunities are considered, as is the stability of their relationships and the home life style. The children's home conditions, health, behavior, and overall environment are also important.

To examine the progress of children in school or their medical records when living with one particular custodial parent requires a subpoena.

Witnesses in child custody cases often include physicians, neighbors, friends, babysitters, and teachers. They can all give testimony about the general cleanliness, appearance, dress, and behavior of the children, as well as their relations with their parents.

Investigation reports completed by private investigators rely on court documents, records, and photographs to prove evidence. They should be obtained to help determine the best interest of the children. A person seeking custody should have good, stable employment in a good occupation field. The person needs to show the length of his

Hoover's surveillance SUV has dark tinted windows. The open back door exposes the camera on a tripod.

Hoover photographing evidence on foot while hidden in a bushy area

employment, the hours worked, the pay, and prior employment and reason for leaving. It is also important to explain how long the person is absent from the home and provide 10 years of residency history. Reports list the family's social activities in clubs, churches, hobbies, sports and friends, including drug and alcohol use. They also include the amount of parent's time spent with their children per week and their activities with them.

Professionals, such as psychiatrists, psychologists, social workers, counselors and clergy give expert testimony in child custody cases. Custody issues are traumatic for all involved, and litigation is very costly. The process is especially hard on children. If the outcome is the replacement of the child's custodial parent, it is done in the best interest of the child in order to provide a safe, stable, healthy environment filled with love and care. Custody changes can be based on the children's exposure to drugs, alcohol, mental or physical abuse, unhealthy conditions, or a dirty or bad environment. If a parent is unable to financially care for a child, has an unstable home life, moves often, drives under the influence of alcohol, or has many sexual relationships, those factors can influence a child custody case.

Domestic Surveillance
and a .357 Magnum

Mel Hoover, private investigator, worked hand-in-hand with some local attorneys. One in particular was an up-coming prominent defense attorney in criminal defense and personal injury cases. His firm's in-house investigator was a long time friend of Hoover. The firm usually contacted Hoover in all domestic matters.

One day the attorney made contact with Hoover and told him to drop everything immediately and go directly to the residence of his client and make arrangements to conduct investigation surveillance with photos. Hoover did just that. The client said his estranged wife was secretly taking items from his residence using numerous people to help. He needed photographic evidence as soon as possible. Upon locating the residence, Hoover noticed it was on a very secluded private road and the house was set way back under some high Fir trees on private grounds.

Hoover assessed the situation and hid his car on a side street. The only way to get photographs quickly in the situation was on foot. He walked to the private road and observed the surroundings and environmental conditions. He walked half way down the driveway adjacent to the intersecting main street. He observed the female subject, identifying her by the description and photograph provided by her spouse. She was with a group of men. They were all loading household goods and appliances into a pickup truck backed up to the house. Hoover took photographs with a 35 mm camera equipped with a stubby 300 mm telephoto lens. He took pictures of the vehicle and its Washington license plates. He also took photos of the female subject and her male companions loading the truck with items.

Just as he completed snapping the photographs, he observed out of the corner of his eye a vehicle driving by. It drove very slowly as if to turn into the private drive, but drove on past it. Hoover immediately figured he'd been busted. He began walking away from the private road and down to the intersecting street. He observed the vehicle return and drive directly to the residence where the female target was loading the truck.

The driver in the car apparently told about his presence because as Hoover looked back, he noted all the men from the truck were running up the private road toward him at a very fast clip. The man in the lead was carrying a .357 magnum Smith & Wesson revolver and pointed it towards Hoover. They caught up quickly to Hoover who was just walking at a fast pace. Hoover was confronted by the man and his cohorts. Mel observed the man's body language, facial expressions, demeanor and tone of his voice.

Hoover made a verbal note of the weapon's presence to the group and attempted to keep them talking. He persuaded the gun wielder to put the weapon away. Hoover kept his eagle eye on the gun until it was in the man's rear waistband. Hoover began a line of questioning relating to the weapon and their aggressive behavior.

He asked the man if there was a need to have the gun. Hoover further said, "There is no need for violence. Can we all calm down?"

The group did not calm down. The group of men made a slight circle around Hoover. The first male, being the leader and confident since he had the gun in his possession, was losing his temper because of the investigator's actions. He lunged at Mel in an attempt to get the camera from under Hoover's coat. He wanted to destroy the film to do away with the evidence. Hoover used foot work and hand blocks as evasive tactics to deflect the man's attempt to grab the camera. He displayed confidence and physical agility to the group which made them back off.

Hoover then distanced himself somewhat from the group. The gun wielder started to walk away. Hoover took out his camera and took a picture of the gun in the man's waist band for additional proof.

This aggravated the subject again, and he made another attempt to assault Mel. Hoover once again used evasive tactics and rendered the attack unsuccessful. The investigator assumed a defensive position a safe distance away from the man again and took mental notes of the assailant's physical description. The group finally walked away, making verbal threats and demanding that the investigator leave the area at once.

Mel Hoover immediately utilized the pre-planned escape route and contacted the Pierce County Sheriff's department. However they were on strike and did not respond. They only took his verbal report over the phone. They were happy that his ability to defuse the situation had caused the leader to put away his gun, Hoover continued on the escape route and was able to depart the area without further incident.

The group broke up because of the investigator's actions in keeping the group talking instead of attacking. His evasive tactics also prevented the gang from attacking him and prevented him from receiving bodily harm. Consequently, the evidence was preserved and protected. The pre-planned escape plan assured him of leaving as quickly as possible from the scene and saved his life.

The evidence was presented to the attorney and his client. A background investigation was conducted on the gun-wielding male subject, revealing that he was dishonorably discharged from the U.S. Air Force because of an assault. He was later charged for gun possession and intimidation with a weapon. Simple assault and intimidation with a weapon charges were brought forth by the attorney. Do to all the evidence in the matter, the divorce and assault cases were a success. Case closed.

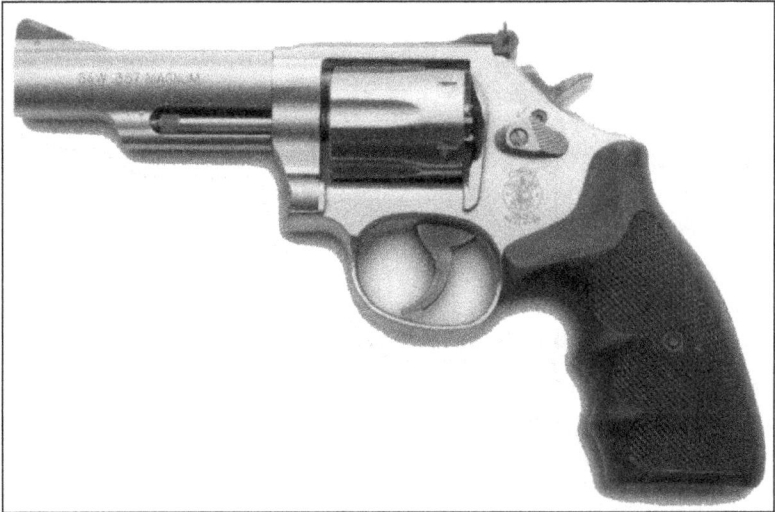

Likeness of weapon carried by the assailant

Criminal Defense of
Attempted Murder Case "Racial"

On one Fall day, investigator Mel Hoover was to meet prospective clients at their middle-class residence. They were a family of "Montana Indians" who came to the Northwest and purchased their home in Tacoma, Washington. They were resented by some people in the neighborhood. They were dedicated family members. The father, who was up in years, was deaf and had been a rodeo bronco rider. He currently worked as a janitor for a local bank. The mother stayed at home to raise her daughter who was attending college. They had two sons, one in college and the other working as a janitor. None of the family members drank alcohol or smoked.

Hoover met with them and discussed an harassment case against the next door neighbors. Several neighbors gave testimony that in fact the next door neighbor had been harassing the Indian family. While written affidavits were obtained from them, numerous other neighbors were fearful about becoming involved.

On several evenings, Hoover's surveillance team attempted to stop and apprehend people sneaking about the family's home and firing bee-bee guns at the house. They learned that teenagers had been given money to perform the acts. No one would offer to stand up to prosecute those individuals. By interviewing community members, Hoover learned that the next door neighbor was behind the whole idea. But no one wanted to become involved because of fear that those people would come after them.

Prior to hiring Mel Hoover, the family called the Tacoma police numerous times about harassments and threats. The harassments stopped for a period of time, but there was still tension between the neighbors. Threats and harassments continued privately over the fence that separated the two homes.

Another investigation was launched by the Indians. It discovered that the harassing neighbors drank heavily and frequented a local bar. An undercover operation in the bar determined that during their heavy drinking sessions, they told the bartender that they were going to get rid of their neighbors one way or another. Photographs were obtained of them drinking. However no one would own up to the information or get involved or sign any affidavits regarding the matter.

Harassing neighbors plotting against the Indians inside a local tavern hang out

The harassing neighbor's son dry-firing a gun towards the Indian family's residence

Hoover's documentation on the retired couple showed that they drank beer and wine combinations night and day at the local bar. He also documented numerous parties at their home. Police were summoned at various times because their acts directed at their Indian neighbors. The retired couple also made trouble over their property line in a boundary dispute. So the families had to go to court over the issue. The neighbors attempted every tactic to force the family to move from the community and proceeded to inspire a conspiracy.

The conspiracy had been proven in prior investigations. It had been festering, multiplying and compounding. The Indian family was tense, stressed out, and in fear for their lives. It had gone on year after year, ever since they moved into the community. On this particular year, a shooting occurred.

On that particular day, it was fairly nice. The sun was out briefly and the air was warm with a slight overcast. There was a party going on in the back yard at the retired couple's home, as usual. The retired couple and their son and his girl friend, both in their 30s, were intoxicated in the secluded back yard. The son was an ex-con.

The Indian family was in their back yard hanging out their laundry on the clothes line. The neighboring father and son had a hand gun they displayed. They took turns with the 45 caliber automatic dry firing it at their neighbors. The family was terrified and in fear for their lives. The neighbors repeated the dry firing even when they returned inside their home. They dry fired at the building and pointed directly at the windows where the Indians were standing. The family summoned the police who spoke with the neighbors. As soon as the police left, it started all over again.

Several weeks later under similar circumstances, the father and son brought out the weapon into the back yard and dry fired it at the Indian family. They were seen drinking beer. One of the Indian family sons went upstairs and took a photo of the man dry firing at them and their home.

The party was quiet in the back yard for awhile when they went inside their home. Several hours later, in the late afternoon, the Indian family's oldest son was enjoying the sunset on his front porch. He enjoyed the out doors and our great Northwest weather. He had just completed cleaning and reloading a 45 model Western style six shooter revolver. He laid it on a small outdoor table on the porch. He was sitting in an adjacent chair, chilling out and looking at the sunset.

The retired couple's son came out of the front door of his mother's home and walked towards his vehicle parked in front of the home. As he walked, he saw the Indian on his front porch and began giving verbal threats and middle finger gestures to him. He got in his vehicle and started it. He began to leave very slowly past the Indian family's house and yelled profanity and made more middle finger gestures. The Indians' son stood up. The old pickup truck stopped directly in front of the Indians' front door.

The driver exited his truck and made further verbal insults and racial slurs. He walked briskly towards the picket fence entrance gate to the front yard. The gate's latch was locked. He kicked the gate wide open and walked briskly forward on the sidewalk towards the front door where the Indian was standing. The Indian yelled loudly for him to stop right there, to make an about face, and leave now. He did not. He came at the Indian on the porch. He was wearing a blue pull-over sweatshirt and blue jeans. He had his right hand under his sweat shirt indicating he might have a gun underneath. The Indian yelled one final time for him to halt and leave now. The man did not respond to the orders, but kept on coming. The Indian then reached over and picked up his revolver and began firing.

The first bullet stuck him in the right shoulder, spinning him around. He went backwards to the gate and fell down. More shots were fired. He managed to keep low as he got up and made his way around to the back side of the truck. More shots rang out, one after another. The victim zig zagged across the street and disappeared from sight.

The Indian had fired all six shots at him but struck him only once. The victim managed to make it over to the next street and to a neighbor's house. He went to the front door and knocked. When the door opened, the victim fell into the living room and spilled his blood there. The neighbor dialed 9-1-1 for police and an ambulance. The neighbor stopped the bleeding as much as possible until the ambulance arrived and took him to the hospital. He recovered from his wounds.

The police arrived and arrested the Indian for attempted murder. After posting bail, he returned home to his family.

The family was deeply upset and contacted Mel Hoover. Hoover investigated the shooting and searched for another weapon with a metal detector. He found none. However, he did have the documented evidence of prior threats and harassment by the neighbors and their son. He recommended a defense attorney to the family and gave the attorney that information.

The attorney was Hoover's long-time friend for whom he had worked locating witnesses and doing domestic cases. The Indian family retained him to defend the criminal case against their son. He compiled all the facts and information for trial.

At the trial, the attorney used all the facts and details Hoover had provided and convinced the jury that there was reasonable doubt. He argued the shooting was justifiable, and the jury agreed. They found the Indian boy innocent of all charges. He also avoided obtaining a criminal record.

The son went on to school and took criminal courses. After graduating, he became a police officer. He went to the police academy for law enforcement training. After receiving his certificate of completion, he became a deputy for the local Indian tribe on its reservation. His sister is going to college to become a lawyer. It ended well for all. However, there was still tension between the neighbors, but the harassing stopped. Each family kept to themselves with no more confrontations.

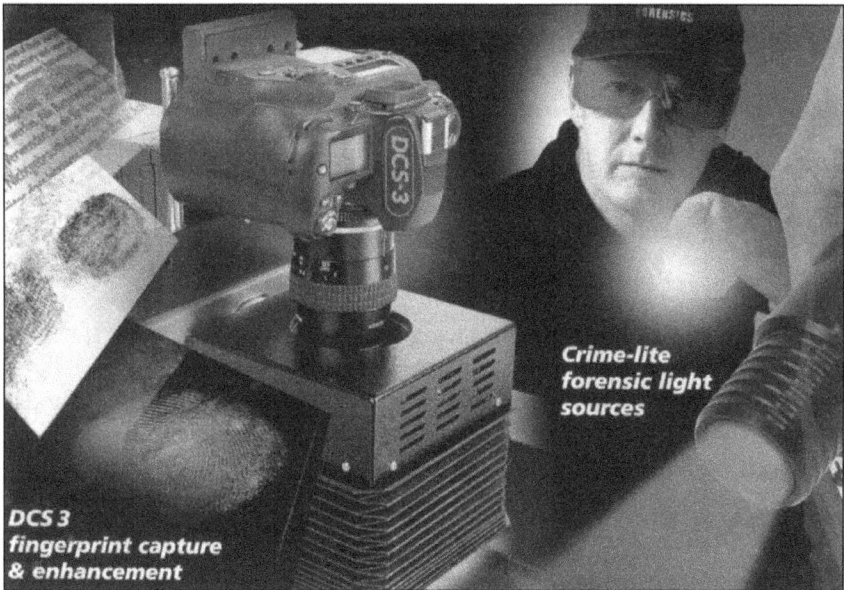

Crime-lite forensic light sources

DCS 3 fingerprint capture & enhancement

Con Artist – Cult Tactics

Investigator Hoover was called upon by a concerned mother and grandmother to investigate the daughter and son-in-law. He received a retainer and arranged for an associate agent to begin the investigation in Hawaii.

The investigator reported to Hoover regarding the married couple with a son. He confirmed the couple was still married but were separated. The daughter was living in military quarters with her son. The son had migraine headaches from time to time and had been hospitalized in the military hospital on occasions.

The son-in-law was an Air Force officer and pilot. The investigator learned that he had committed a crime and was awaiting sentencing to go to a federal prison. His personal problems with his family involved several women. The investigator obtained the name of one woman who lived in Seattle.

Hoover's agency located her residence and gathered intelligence information on her background. They learned she was married to an aircraft engineer working for a large aircraft company in Seattle. Their house was a large, two-story house overlooking Elliot Bay. The husband was involved with classic cars and owned several. He attended all the classic car events in the area. Their relationship was not good, and each went their separate ways. The wife was deeply involved with church and social events and counseled people who were weak and in emotional stress about their needs and wants. She went to various churches seeking out such people. Investigators learned of five people who were victims of her scams to obtain their assets legally. She had great con artist abilities using cult methods. She had studied mind control and used it in conjunction with her spiritual background to enforce her control of people's minds.

Her practice involved using great mind control with a spiritual flavor to enforce her control. The religious guide lines were a stepping stone into controlling a person's mind. The power of religion and mind control proved to be powerful tactics on people who were down and out and in need of help.

The investigators learned her method of operation. She'd seek out troubled, religious people who were mentally weak and in need of guidance. She probed into their backgrounds to learn about their assets and their weak points with their families. She worked on their weak points and over time gained control. With this brain washing, she gained complete control of people. She was like a guru whose primary aim was to obtain legal control over their assets. She had been labeled as a woman guru who became a legal con artist. Her methods were of cult fashion. She zoomed in on her prey to begin her body and mind control.

She was a controller of mind and body. She sought people with weakness or depression who had problems such as marital difficulties. The growth of leaders like her has become large and phenomenal. They're known as gurus. All religions need a prophet and ministers. People's emotional growth and difficulties have created an opportunity for con artists. BS in need of BSers. A guru for every movement. A movement for each guru. Therefore, body psychology is mind control and it can be classified as a disease. It appears our society may be in for an epidemic. This woman knew the ropes. It is big business with big bucks being obtained legally.

The suspect had legally taken away assets of victims. They simply just gave them to her. A couple victims were discovered by investigation interviews. They said they turned over power of attorney to the woman, so in due course, she obtained large sums of money, vehicles, and other properties. Her technique was within the guidelines of the law, so therefore no charges were ever filed against her. Basically, the people willingly and voluntarily gave her their assets.

The Hoover investigation into the "guru" con artist produced a profile report on the subject that they sent to an investigator in Hawaii. The investigation continued there where the son-in-law of Hoover's client was an Air Force officer who was in the stockade awaiting transfer to federal prison. The con artist had worked with his wife during her troubled marriage to the officer. She tried to separate the couple and to obtain his assets from the wife. She failed to do so.

Before the officer was taken into custody, the investigator learned the con artist had also had several sessions with him while he was in prison. During an interview, the officer told the investigator that the guru claimed to be a prophet and saw into the spirit realm. She said the Lord was calling upon him to be an apostle. During sessions that lasted up to 10-12 hours, he sat in a stuffed chair as she probed his mind and body. She claimed she would cleanse his soul and stop him from drinking alcohol and using tobacco. She said his marriage would be saved and his son would have no more terrible headaches.

The investigator also learned the woman had administered the drug Perphanazine, used for mental illness involving brain function, to relax him so she could work on his mind. She coached him on conversations with his wife. She also chanted, and the officer joined in. She talked about things that hurt him deeply, and he would go into depression and commence to cry. She insisted he needed to be saved and played cassette tapes over and over, hours on end to him. She also had him give her very large sums of money and then obtained power of attorney and took all his money. That left him broke in the stockade awaiting trial and transfer to federal prison. The con artist told him she would be a character witness for him at trial.

The officer became so brain washed that he called this guru "mom." She had his head spinning. His marriage fell apart. He had a girl friend during this time, and the con artist tried to brain wash his girl friend, too, but failed. She continued to work on the officer to discourage him from marrying the girl friend. She screamed her chantings at the top of her voice. She stated that evil spirits' manipulations were behind all wedding vows. She said that all he knew and cared about were sexual activities. That was his happiness. She said all he wanted to do is screw. She asked, "Don't you see that the Lord's power is within me? You defy God, you defy me."

At the officer's trial, the woman did testify as a character witness as promised. She also made up stories that were out-and-out lies. In trying to save him from prison, she lied about certain events relating to the crime. However he was found guilty in the court trial and sentenced to on year in federal prison and received a dishonorable discharge from the Air Force.

The officer's wife left Hawaii and went to Seattle with her son. They lived in a rented home. The con artist also returned to Seattle where investigators followed the case. They kept the client, the wife's mother, abreast of what was happening. The con artist contacted the wife again and tried to get inside her head but failed.

People at the con artist's Seattle church had heard rumor about her activities in Hawaii. They approached her and asked numerous questions. She would say the she was working for God on a mission to help the officer and his family. She said, "No help from God or me could save them. He was not being right with himself or others, including his family."

Her brain washing, cult tactics made her a legal con artist. She took thousands of dollars from her followers/victims. She lived like a queen in the best of clothing and cars. She traveled and had money in the bank. She smiled all the way to her bank. From the officer, she was drawing $1,900 monthly that was automatically deposited into her bank account, just by use of her power of attorney.

Federal investigators learned from Hoover's investigation that she had lied in the officer's trial. They conducted their own investigation and obtained evidence that she had committed perjury. They had evidence to prove it. The U.S. Marshalls asked Hoover where the woman was. He directed them to her home where they arrested her for perjury and sent her to jail. The wife was reunited with her mother. The case was closed.

CULTS AND CONS

The Exploitation of the Emotional Growth Consumer

Ritualistic Occultists

There was a Mason County cult group that sought out people 50-years-old and older. A young married couple became very worried about their parents who had drifted apart from them. The parents were retired civil servants who had lost their house because they didn't plan or manage their finances very well. They were stressed out because the children, who had eight children and not enough space in their house, wouldn't take them in. They tried going back to work, but their ages were against them, and that was another crushing blow. They belonged to a local church which gave them help and some hope. However there was a small group which took church members away from the church.

The young couple wanted to learn what was going on with their parents. Were they involved with a cult? They contacted Mel Hoover to investigate. Hoover located the parents who resided with another couple. The parents had become isolated. They were allowed to have no contact with anyone. Hoover interviewed church members and various neighbors. He learned the parents had had no phone contact with anyone. That was not allowed by the small group.

Hoover obtained one of the group's bibles and further learned that every single passage was underlined in red. It was apparently re-written for the group's purposes. The group was led by a "minister" who controlled the group. They had daily sessions in an old barn. Most of the members of the group were up in age and had turned over all their assets to the minister who claimed they would go over to the prophet. The couple, who had some money in a local bank, had also turned it over to the "minister." He used the bible as a tool for his own mission. The members became victims of a scam.

Hoover submitted his report to the young married couple. But during the investigation, another couple asked him if he would investigate another group in the Olympia area. Their teenage daughters had joined a group of teens there and had been cut off from their parents. They felt their daughters had fallen into a life of drugs.

After a month of investigating, Hoover learned the group was located in a secluded country setting. They were residing in a large house there. People said that animals in the area had been mutilated. They also had heard heavy metal music coming from the house and saw numerous candles burning late into the night there. They reported various sighting of Satanic symbols in the area and of seeing the teenage group playing games in the surrounding wooded areas.

The police had been notified and had investigated, but occult activities are not in themselves illegal. No crime had been committed.

Neighbors reported hearing heavy metal music with satanic lyrics while the group played Dungeons and Dragons. Investigators learned that most of the group were true believers. The daughters dabbled reading their literature and collected incense, knives, chalices, candles and other cult paraphernalia. They were being influenced by the group activities and used drugs.

The investigation team conducted surveillance. They happened to catch the two teen-aged daughters by themselves. They apprehended the girls and returned them to their parents who took them to a deprogrammer and to drug rehabilitation. Case closed.

Cults and dollars – money making scams

Spiritualist Warrior and Gay Husband

Investigator Hoover was called by a law firm and referred to a spiritualist client of theirs. The client lived in Thurston County on a large ranch that kept Arabian horses. The beautiful, large horses were given the best of care in a very nice barn and stables that included shower stalls. The main house was large and spread out among the horse acreage. The ranch was fenced and had a security gate for entry and exit. Hoover contacted the spiritualist's security personnel and they provided him information about the assigned case. The security service patrolled the grounds and kept unauthorized people from entering the property. They also provided security for everyone on the premises.

The female client was very beautiful with blonde hair streaming down her backside. She had become famous in her spiritual teachings. A 30,000-year-old warrior appeared within her body and related to others how to live life. Her new age spiritual techniques were known all over the world. Many of her followers were well off financially and included several well known female movie stars.

The investigation focused on the spiritualist's ex-husband who had divorced her. He was dissatisfied with the divorce settlement. Hoover learned he was spreading rumors about her, saying that she was a fake and was scamming people for their money. She, in turn, had arranged various tests of her warrior sessions which proved she wasn't a fake and wasn't scamming people.

The investigation placed her ex-husband under surveillance. They determined he was living with a male partner who was behind the ex-husband during court proceedings where he sought more financial support for the two living together. It came out that the ex-husband had AIDS and was gay. In addition to more financial support, he was out to get revenge and destroy his ex-wife completely.

The investigation and surveillance produced all the facts for the court proceedings. It came down to a win/lose situation, so a settlement was reached. The ex-husband later died of AIDS. The spiritualist had no bitter feelings or hatred towards him. She was tested negative for AIDS and continued with her work.

Hoover was contacted for another investigation where there appeared to be a conspiracy going on involving a female member of the local church of this same small community. The spiritualist brought many followers to the community. The town grew, there were more jobs, and it became very stable financially. The spiritualist supported the local schools and awarded money for students' college scholarships. But one church pastor claimed her teachings were that of a "cult."

During the investigation, Hoover learned a local church was loosing members. They were joining this new age group of spiritualists instead. The pastor was concerned that she ran a cult that never taught anything about religion or about God. The ranch was classified as a compound and had armed guards. He alleged that she brainwashed her followers and held them against their will. The news media jumped on the band wagon but later helped expose these false rumors.

The investigators had a tour of the whole facility, including the barn, main house, guest houses, and even the fruit cellar which was rumored to be a dungeon. The spiritualist also wanted the entire establishment debugged. The whole premises was gone over from top to bottom. No hidden listening devices were found anywhere. There was no evidence found of a gun room or any guns. Investigators found no people being held against their will, and did not find a dungeon or a maze.

The rumors mentioned on particular girl who was being held against her will and was being brain washed. She was shown on television and supposedly had to be re-programmed because of the teachings of the cult. However the investigation learned the woman was tied in with the church's conspiracy theory designed to destroy the teachings of the spiritualist-warrior's. No evidence of a cult was found. The spiritualist's new-age teaching sessions were about God and his love. They focused on how to love yourself and succeed in life, how to be good and be a good neighbor. It turned out that the church was basically losing members and money and were very fearful of the new age religious power. So they began the rumors.

There was not enough hard evidence to establish slander for a libel suit, and the client did not want to pursue one.

Out of concern that some people were outside listening to the spiritualist's teaching sessions, a team of investigators scanned the area for anyone listening or interfering with wireless frequencies to disrupt the sessions. The concern was unfounded and everything was clear.

Investigators heard the teaching sessions. They were held in the large, open barn. She used a wireless microphone that transmits over a special frequency to surrounding speakers. During her teachings, the 30,000-year-old warrior enters her body and converses with members

The Arabian horse ranch owned and operated by a female spiritualist, near a small, local town

This beautiful spiritualist woman, with many followers, contacts a 30,000-year-old ancient warrior that takes over her body and soul. He therefore speaks out with wisdom for a spiritualist life.

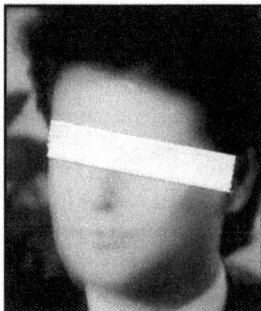

The gay husband sought revenge so he sued his ex-wife for money to treat his AIDS disease

about God, love, and how to succeed in life. There was nothing said against God or any type of brain washing going on. They were just as normal as in any church setting teaching the bible or about God. But her teachings had become steeped in harsh ritual and in fear.

The spiritualist's membership was well over 1,000 young people and growing. Her techniques have become known all over the world. Despite the mud slinging and sharp arrows thrown at this famous spiritualist, her teachings have touched many people, including movie stars. People choose to believe it or not, just as anyone chooses to believe in any religion. Case closed.

Spiritual teachings:
"Love yourself. Be good to yourself."

God / Jesus really not mentioned in their teachings. Only messages received are from a 30,000-year-old warrior, who apparently, maybe, connected with God as is portrayed in their spiritual teaching sessions.

Lesbian Activities

One sunny summer day, investigator Hoover met with a very prominent timber king who was having family problems. He wanted to conduct a domestic investigation of his wife. He said that one of his daughters came home from the University of Washington one weekend. As she entered the home, she began looking for her mother. She couldn't find her anywhere, so she went to the master bedroom. The door was closed. When she opened it, low and behold she saw her mother sitting on the bed with another woman and partially undressed. They had been embracing one another. The daughter became very upset and asked, "What in the hell is going on here?" There was no reply. The daughter told everyone in her family about the situation she had uncovered.

She had three brothers and two sisters, all attending the University of Washington. The timber king told Hoover that he had talked over the situation with his children and his wife. However, it appeared that the relationship was still going on between the two women.

He said they had been married forty years and that retirement was just a couple years away. He said that his business trips kept them separated for periods of time and that his wife's involvement in community organizations and clubs kept her from accompanying him on his trips. He admitted that he had neglected their time together, and he felt very responsible for the situation.

The family's male gardener had been with them for years. He had been away from his sister for years. One day he contacted her in Eastern Washington and invited her over for a visit. When she arrived, he introduced her to the family. They became friends and started socializing and going out together frequently. They spent more and more time together. The timber baron noticed a change in his wife, but he could not put his finger on what was happening. Unbeknownst to him, his wife was spending every spare moment with the gardener's sister. He told Hoover he wanted proof about what was going on. He said the woman had moved to Western Washington and was selling herbal vitamins. He said his wife had spent thousands of dollars on those products.

The father and his children supported one another in this situation. They decided to hire several out-of-state psychiatrists who were the best in their field. They held therapy sessions with the wife, but she made up stories and lied regarding her involvement with the gardener's sister. She was in a state of denial. The family could provide the psychiatrists no documented evidence about the wife's behavior from which they could work. So they paid Hoover a retainer to get some facts and documentation for the doctors.

The background investigation began on the gardener's sister. Hoover learned that she and her brother were born in a small town in Eastern Washington. Their parents were farmers. She was a loner in childhood and liked being a Tom-boy. In her teens, she did not date boys. On occasion, she went out with female companions, however. Hoover eventually obtained documented evidence that the woman was a lesbian.

He submitted his report to the client. He was very upset and the children were fit to be tied. They placed an illegal telephone recorder on their phone line and learned that the relationship between the two women had blossomed even while the wife attended the psychiatric sessions. Not only was the relationship growing stronger and stronger, but the woman was using methods of speech to control the mother. She also squeezed thousands of dollars from their mother.

The family wanted the relationship stopped now. The children located the lesbian's hiding place and went there to confront her. They harassed her with threats and told her she had better stop seeing their mother now! The children also confronter their mother and insisted she stop seeing this woman. Despite these attempts, the women managed to slip out and see one another.

The family was very distressed and emotionally upset. They summoned Hoover to a family meeting and told him they wanted the relationship stopped now. They offered him a million dollars to make the problem disappear. They said they wanted the woman eliminated, abducted, or drowned with no trace in American Lake. Hoover had a long serious talk with them. He set them straight on their thoughts, behavior, and actions concerning their mother's relationship.

Hoover continued the investigation. He noted that since the family confronted their mother that her lesbian partner had moved to a new location. He located her new residence which was not too far from the family's home. It was a small house in a small cubby hole surrounded by a grove of trees and bushes.

The family told Hoover that their mother was still receiving frequent phone calls after which she would disappear. They knew the calls were from the lesbian. Hoover told them the woman had complete control over their mother by the power of suggestion and on the strength of their relationship. She was very powerful in her mind control, brain washing tactics. She would call the mother, make a suggestion, and the mother would comply.

Hoover suggested the need to conduct surveillance to verify their activities together. He said that would help the psychiatrists. The family was beginning to lose hope that their mother would stop seeing the woman. They felt her relationship was not normal nor correct in the eyes of God. The father and children agreed on this point, and surveillance was to start immediately.

Hoover continued surveillance for months. He obtained still photographs and video showing the lesbian in affectionate contact with the timber baron's wife. He photographed them holding hands and kissing. He also obtained photos of the hotels and motels they used, and of them coming and going for days on end and of the lesbian driving the mother's new BMW two-door sedan.

Hoover presented his report and photographs and videos to the family and the psychiatrists. The evidence allowed the psychiatrists to have a good handle on her activities so that she could no longer lie to them in sessions about where she was and with whom. The surveillance documented her activities each day and evening.

The family began working together as a whole with the psychiatrists. The surveillance was a very useful tool in working with the mother. The family began to have hope that the mother was coming around during her treatment sessions with the doctors.

Months later, everyone noticed a great improvement in her.

Hoover's report and documenting photographs and video had a great impact. The mother and wife could not lie any longer about her outings with her lesbian partner. Denying her actions and behavior became a thing of the past. The truth prevailed, and the brain washing hold on the mother was broken.

Later, as the mother improved further in treatment sessions, she realized what she was doing and how it affected her marriage and her relationships with her children, friends and relatives. She eventually broke off all contact with the lesbian. She went back to being a normal spouse and mother with a deep love for her husband and children.

The investigation ended and so did the mother's psychiatric sessions. They became a happy family together. The timber baron husband settled down and spent more time at home with his wife and had great adventures together. Case closed.

Injury Accident Investigation

Investigator Hoover was contacted by a law firm to conduct an investigation on a personal injury case. A woman had fallen in a stairwell while looking at a business location that was for sale. She wanted to relocate her beauty salon to a better location. On a bright, sunny day she went to the building which was located on a high-traffic street. She parked her vehicle adjacent to the building and entered the building. The owner had let her in to inspect it. He then had to leave for a moment. He told her to check out the building and that he'd be right back.

She looked over the main floor, which suited her needs. There was a downstairs for storage, so she began walking down the steps. She slipped and then tumbled down the stairwell. She lay there with terrific pain in her back. She couldn't move at all or even cry out. The owner returned and found her lying at the base of the stairwell. He called 911, and she was rushed to the hospital. She had broken her back, a spine injury that could cost her the ability to walk again.

Hoover began the investigation by gaining access to the building. He looked about then inspected the stairwell. He determined the composition and construction of the steps. He noted the height, width, and depth of the stairs. He determined that all the steps were equal. He located the step where the woman had slipped and found it to be unstable, wobbly, and smooth. It had no nosing on it.

The stairway was straight with no curves. The floor at the base was concrete. He noted the location where the victim had landed, and took measurements. He also noted that there was no handrail on the stairs, which did not conform to local or state building code requirements. He found no obstructions on the stairway. He took photographs and made diagrams of the scene, including the wobbly step and other items relevant to building code requirements.

Hoover interviewed other prospective buyers who also remembered the wobbly step. A couple said they had stumbled a bit on the step, but managed to keep from falling. Hoover learned from witnesses he interviewed that they had informed the owner of the wobbly step, but that he took no action to repair it. He also gave no warnings about the step to prospective buyers looking at the building. Hoover obtained affidavits from several witnesses, several of whom said they had almost fallen on the step. When an accident finally did occur, the victim ended up with a very serious back injury.

Hoover submitted his report to the attorney. The firm filed a lawsuit against the owner and his insurance company. The litigation resulted in an out-of-court settlement, and the case was closed.

Analysis: Computer drawings of accident scene

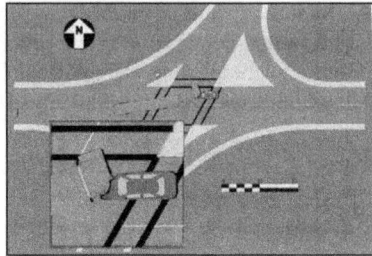

Collision diagrams – the new way

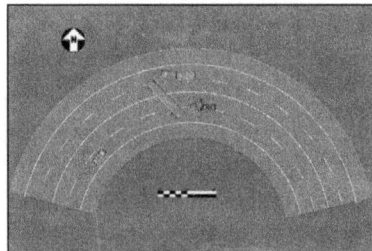

Vehicle Accident Investigation

Investigator Hoover was called by a large law firm that specialized in personal injury vehicle accidents. He met with the attorney handling one such case. The attorney had a police report and some details of the case. The firm filed a personal injury case against the city of Puyallup. The attorney wanted to know more information about the street where the vehicle accident happened. He needed witnesses supporting evidence about the conditions in order to help the victim of the accident, the teenage driver.

Hoover went to the scene of the accident. It was a well known road in Puyallup in a country setting. The street was very long and went up a steep grade to the top where there was a sharp, hair-pin turn to the right. Hoover canvassed the area, talking to neighbors about the road. They said it was well known that teenagers sped up and down the road and minor accidents from time to time also caused by the road condition. Complaints had been called in to the police. They tried to stop the speeding by setting up radar traps. Many tickets were issued. But the neighbor's main complaint was that this was a very dangerous road that needed paving, warning signs, and other repairs.

Hoover obtained statements and signed affidavits about the road conditions from the neighbors. The attorney issued subpoenas to obtain complaint records neighbors had filed with the city about the road.

The investigator obtained supporting documentation that further determined that the street was well used as a main street. It intersected with the long county road at the top of the steep hill. He obtained the slope of the hill along with supporting photographs. He determined the length of the road, from the bottom to the top where the accident happened. Going down this hill in a car at any speed gave one a roller-coaster ride effect. At the end, the bottom portion of the road was covered with loose dirt and gravel. As you drove up the road, about half way up, it became covered with asphalt to the very top, where it made a 90-degree turn toward the county line. Hoover measured and photographed the road.

The county's portion of the road marked with curve signs and slow signs. As one come down the hill from the county line and past the 90-degree curve, the road began a downward descent. The city had no signs as you moved down the hill or beginning at the curve. No warning signs of any kind regarding the steep grade or its hazards were posted on the city's portion of the road. No sign warned of the abrupt end of the asphalt and the beginning of loose dirt and gravel half way down the street.

During his investigation, Hoover learned that during a bright June evening, teenagers who were graduating from high school, were out joy riding and celebrating the next night's graduation ceremonies. They were all jolly and in a very happy state of mind. Their car was a 1970 Chevrolet 2-door coup. It was in very good condition. There were no defects in the tires, brakes, engine or the body. The teenage driver, his girlfriend, and his best friend in the back seat, were driving on this same road. They had just made the 90-degree turn at the top of the road and were going down the city's hill. The car picked up speed as it descended and gave them a good roller-coaster ride. It was calculated that they were traveling about 45-50 mph on this asphalted portion of the road with no warning signs. As the car hit the dirt and gravel section of the road, it began to fish-tail, an eye witness said. The driver lost control of the car and locked up the brakes as it slid off the west side of the road and over a slight embankment. The car rolled over and landed upright with extensive roof damage. The driver and both passengers were thrown around inside the car and were all injured.

Witnesses went to the car to assist and called 911. The ambulance arrived, but they did not remove anyone from the car. The police found one unopened beer can at the scene. Their investigation report indicated the driver had been speeding and may have been drinking.

The passengers were removed from the car, placed in the ambulance, and taken to Puyallup's hospital. The driver had a broken neck, but the passengers only ended up with cuts and bruises and were released from the hospital. A blood test was performed on the driver, who was in critical condition. The test showed the driver had not been drinking and had no other drugs in his body.

The driver ended up being a quadriplegic. His parents hired the law firm which filed a negligence suit against the city, alleging the road was unsafe and did not have any warning signs.

Hoover's investigation obtained photographs of road conditions, neighbors' statements, police reports on their attempts to slow down speeders, calls about vehicle mishaps on the road, tow truck records, neighbors' complaints to the city council about the dangerous road, measurements, diagrams, road maintenance records, and witness' statements. His report showed conclusively that the city was negligent. After the lawsuit was filed, the city settled with the boy's family out of court. Case closed.

An accident scene – vehicle collision

Game Warden Missing Persons Homicide

Mel Hoover was called to search for and investigate the case of two missing persons. It was in the dead of winter and snow was coming down in the mountains and surrounding areas. The client was an old friend of Hoover's. He had retired from the Washington State Department of Game, where he had been a top-notch game warden and a state game trapper. Exhibitions of his game were displayed yearly at the Puyallup Fair grounds. His niece was a federal customs agent on Tacoma's tide flats. He had one son, and his wife was deceased. He and his son lived in the city of Puyallup on acreage. He had a large, old, two-story home and he farmed the land around it. He also did lawn mower repairs.

The warden's son was ex-Navy, just like his father. He tried to be somewhat like his father. He obtained a state trapper's license. His father turned the trap lines over to him. They skinned the animals and dried their hides for market. The father and son both liked the outdoor life, hunting and fishing, and animals. The son also obtained a commercial fishing license. He sold fish and animal pelts. The father and son worked together, and after the mother died, their relationship became closer. The father taught the son about fishing, trapping, and selling both. They were somewhat close, but his father really never knew much about the son's social life except that he played in a band in Auburn, WA. He had several girl friends, with one of whom he had a child. The father really didn't know what the son did in the evenings. The money they earned went into a joint bank account. When the son needed money, he'd always come to his father. The son's main occupation was as a roofer.

The son's main girlfriend lived with her mother and his two-year-old daughter in an apartment. The son paid support for his child, but his relationship with her was very, very stormy. It was on and off. They both went their separate ways at times, but she always chased him and ended up back in the picture. He did the same thing. The boy's father told him to stay away from the girlfriend because she was bad news. The girlfriend's mother told her the same thing. They fought at the apartment. The police were summoned, but no charges were filed. They had argued, slapped one another, and supposedly threatened each other. Another time, he made a forced entry into the mother's apartment and went after his girl friend. Puyallup police were called, and domestic violence charges were filed and a restraining

The game warden father searched for his son after his son's girl friend was murdered in the mountains near Elbe, Washington. Investigator Mel Hoover was assigned to the case.

Still missing today, Mike, the son, was a suspect in the killing of his girl friend. Her 2-year-old daughter was found at the K-Mart store in Spanaway, Washington

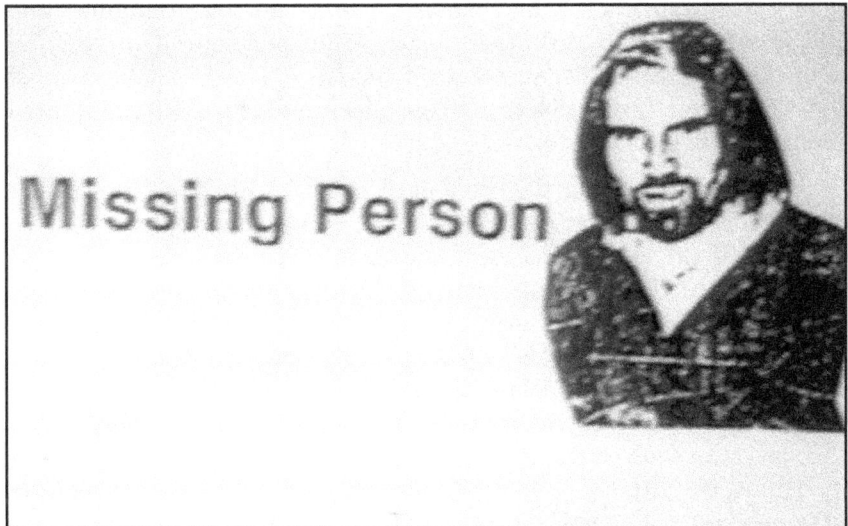

order resulted. However, neither complied with the order. They kept seeing each other, bouncing back and forth from one residence to another. Both were again advised to stay away from one another. The son's father said, "She's nothing but trouble for you."

The investigator, knowing the circumstances, took on the case and began searching and investigating. There were search teams, and the police eventually joined in. The son, his girl friend, and their daughter were together in his truck. He had asked his father for a small amount of money for gas, and received it. After that, they left the father's house for the trap lines to pick up his December catch. It was nearly Christmas, and he was earning money for the holiday season. There had been no roofing jobs because of the winter weather, so he was counting on his trap lines to provide money for gifts. His girl friend had already purchased a gift on a charge card from K-Mart. It was on hold there to be picked up.

The son's pickup truck was a 1980 red Plymouth with a rear canopy. He had a small boat on top. It was early Saturday morning in 1985 when the three of them headed out to the trap lines with the few dollars he had received from his dad. It was cold out, frosty in the low lands and snowing in the mountains. The morning before, the son had received a call from his boss to report to work for a special roofing job on Sunday. He told his boss he'd be there. He told his girlfriend about the extra work as they left in his pickup truck.

Late that evening, the father became worried because his son should have been back hours ago. He called the sheriff's department. His theory was that his son and the girl friend and their daughter had slid off the road in the mountains. Volunteer search teams and investigator Hoover began work on the case. The police broadened the search, too, trying to locate three missing persons. No one located them that day nor the following day.

Hoover began tracking the son's path between his trap lines in the Clark's Creek to Chamber's Creek area. Some women and a child at the edge of the creek said they saw them at Chamber's Creek. The son was in his boat out in the pond retrieving his traps when they saw them. Meanwhile, the two-year-old daughter was found at the Spanaway K-Mart store the day the three disappeared. Nobody knew it was the child of the missing couple. Police took the child, who had bruises and scratches, for treatment. The news media picked up on the story and showed the girl during the news. The girlfriend's mother identified the little girl on television and went to pick her up and take her home. The police questioned the little girl.

Now the search and investigation took a turn. Where was the couple? Was there foul play? Why was the little girl left at the K-Mart? The searches continued each day for weeks. Friends joined in, as did the Pierce County Search and Rescue teams. The rivers were searched. Fort Lewis was searched, Roy, Yelm, the mountain highway from Alder Lake to the entrance to Mt. Rainier, and Highway 7 leading to Morton were searched. They looked around streams, rivers, and ponds where he had trap lines. A bail bondsman who was interested in the case joined the search with Hoover.

Pierce County conducted an air search flying over the trap line route. One search was off of Highway 7. Mike's best friend, who had gone on these trap lines with Mike, guided the pilot to search to the right of the highway. It was cold and the ground was covered with snow. Mike's friend coordinated with the Sheriff's Department in the searches. He was never considered a suspect. However, he guided the searches and was interviewed on television news. Investigator Hoover was suspicious of him. He gathered information about him. He was in a circle of people with Mike which dealt and used drugs. He was also a drug user. He went around with Mike on the trap lines. There was an association of trappers in some of the same areas.

A local psychic was contacted by Mike's relatives. She had a vision of the missing woman lying on the ground, her head pointed in an easterly direction towards Mt. Rainier. Her feet appeared to be in water. This is all she could vision at the time, and Hoover and others obtained that information.

A few days after the psychic's report and after air and ground searches, a discovery was made by a Puyallup man. He and his dog went for a ride near Mt. Rainier, turning onto Highway 7 heading toward Morton. Snow was on the ground. He happened to see an old logging road, so he pulled off onto the road. He drove up it until he could go no further because of the snow and downed tree limbs. He parked his pickup truck and got out with his dog. The dog ran up the old logging road heading northeast, then curving east. He tried to call the dog back because he couldn't keep up.

As he rounded the bend in the road, he saw his dog stopped. He noticed the back end of a red pickup truck with a canopy. Snow was on the roof. As he approached the truck, he saw a woman's body lying face down, her head pointing east toward the mountain. Snow covered her body.

The man notified the Pierce County Sheriff's Department. The following day, Hoover, the bail bondsman, and sheriff's deputies arrived at the scene. The woman was identified as Mike's girl friend, but Mike was not there. Dental records later identified the partially decomposed body as Mike's girl friend. Hoover made notes and observations at the scene. He saw no signs of a struggle on the victim, who was behind the truck. Most evidence had been destroyed by the winter elements. Her body appeared to be nude with her hands tied behind her back. There was also a tube sock tied about her neck. Evidence showed she had been stabbed several times.

After the body had been removed, investigator Hoover observed the red pickup. Through the windowed canopy, he noted lots of trap line game animals inside. He was told that the large number of animals in the truck was a good take for this time of year and that they would have brought a good sum of money if sold. An inventory of items in the truck was taken. Mike's father said that one burlap sack was missing that Mike was going to use, like he used every year at this time, to wrap a Christmas tree from the trap line. A pruning saw used to cut the tree was also missing, as was a 22-caliber revolver, a leather holster with belt, a knife and leather case and a length of heavy chain. It was also said that there was a small black notebook on the truck floor. On the dashboard of the truck was a note Mike had written to his girl friend which said, "I love you." The driver's seat was pushed way back. It appeared that a long-legged person possibly six-feet tall had driven the truck. Mike was short with short legs.

On further observations of the truck, Hoover saw that Mike's warm flannel jacket was in the front seat pushed back against the rear of the seat. Clothing he was wearing on the trap line included Levis, a plaid, long-sleeved shirt, black rubber hip boots. Hoover felt the observations indicated someone else was driving Mike's truck. It was cold and occasionally snowing the day he left, and no one in their right mind would be left without their jacket.

The "I love you" note was verified to have been written in Mike's handwriting. Mike's 86-year-old father said many times that his 36-year-old son had written that note months earlier.

Pierce County detectives turned the investigation over to a Lewis County detective since the homicide happened in that county. The detective was very narrow minded. Hoover spoke to him on several occasions. His mind was focused on Mike as the killer. "He may run, but no one can run forever. He will be caught," said the detective. At the time, Mike was missing. He was a suspect to be questioned. Yet the Lewis County detective would not listen to what Hoover had to say. In theory, Hoover believed Mike was dead prior to his girl friend's death. He was a good hunter and trapper, knowledgeable of the woods. If he wanted to kill her, Hoover felt he could have done it and hidden the body so there would just be a missing person report.

There was more to this case. It just didn't add up. Only the police and the girl friend's mother believed Mike had done it. They wanted justice served. Catch him and punish him to the limits of the law.

Prior to the truck disappearing, Hoover learned that Mike's red pickup truck with a boat on top was seen at the Spanaway K-Mart store at the far end of the parking lot. Next to it was another pickup truck with a canopy and boat on top. There appeared to be two white, bearded males in the second truck. A white woman about 30-years old with blond, neck-length hair and wearing a blouse and Levis walked into the K-Mart with Mike's girl friend, who was wearing the same type of clothing. The girl friend was with a female child about three years of age. The witness identified Mike's girl friend from photographs show to them. They entered the store and left it, but no one remembered if the little girl went with them. Later, the girl was found in the store with no parents.

The police were called. They gathered additional information. Hoover learned the two trucks were seen at four corners in Yelm, one following the other and headed toward the Bald Hills. Witnesses remembered seeing the two trucks on Bald Hills Road heading east passing by the Cedar Estate's entrance. The main road ends but a dirt logging road, called One Thousand Line, continues on. It runs through the base of the Bald Hills Mountains and comes out on the Mountain Highway below Alder Lake.

Other sightings of the two trucks were obtained. They were seen parked next to Alder Lake. The following day, they were seen in Elbe. The crime scene was about 2-1/2 miles from Elbe off of Highway 7 on an abandoned logging road. Mike had traps in near-by streams and in Mineral Lake, all mainly due east from Highway 7.

In the very small town of Elbe, Mike had an association with a well-known drug dealer. Mike and he had a falling out a year or so earlier. Apparently Mike had ratted on him about his drug trafficking and stealing. Nothing became of it, but he maintained a grudge. The Lewis County detective did talk to the drug dealer, but felt there was no connection. The detective felt Mike was in hiding and on the run. However there was something peculiar about the drug dealer in his run-down old home. Just about the time of Mike's disappearance, he poured a concrete slab in the garage area. It appeared as though it was hand mixed and just dumped on the ground and just smoothed out with a shovel, possibly. It was brought to the detective's attention, but he did not pursue the matter. The slab was another connection with Mike's best friend, involving drug dealings.

Pierce County and Lewis County detectives at the crime scene did very extensive searching for Mike and in the area for several days. They even used search dogs. Nothing was found. Hoover's theory was that Mike and his girl friend were overtaken after they left the K-Mart store. The child was brought back and left at the store. Mike could have already been done away with. The girl friend was alive on the route to Yelm, the Bald Hills, Alder Lake, and on Highway 7 to the logging road where she was murdered after a fling with her for several days when she was raped and physically tortured.

The little girl, prior to the finding of her mother's body, said, "Mommy in the trees. Daddy hurt," and "Mommy hurt," indicating mommy was in the truck. No one paid any attention to these words. Focus was maintained on Mike. He was out there and they wanted to talk to him. They put out an all points bulletin for him. There were sightings of look-a-likes. The Lewis County detective thought he was hiding in Alaska. He had a black book that was found on the floor of Mike's truck but he never investigated its contents – the people listed in it. It was believed that the detective returned it back to the girl friend's mother. The detective thought he had his case, cut and dried.

One day the detective and his partner went to Mike's father's home where the father and Hoover tried to talk them into opening their eyes to the case. They just wouldn't listen at all. Their main objective was to look at Mike's old room. They were given permission, and they went through the room like a wind storm. They found Mike's guns, but their interest focused on a piece of rope. It had a knot in it the same as the knot used at the crime scene to tie the girl friend's hands and the tube sock tied about her neck. The detectives left in a hurry and would not sway or listen to the information Hoover and Mike's father had to say.

The father, a ex-game warden, had no contact with his son after he disappeared. He was sure that he was dead. Hoover had the same thoughts. In the past, if there were any type of trouble, Mike would contact his dad. He had no money on him and nobody made contact with the bank regarding his account except for his father, who found all the money was there.

The investigation continued. Hoover confirmed that Mike had an association with various drug people around town. One tavern in Puyallup where Mike played pool was busted for dealing drugs. In Sumner, there was a hang out where drug selling took place in the alley. People entered through the back entrance into the tavern. There was no indication that Mike used drugs, however he may have transported them from one place to another. That was unconfirmed. Mike had a friend he saw frequently in Sumner. The friend had a girl friend Mike also knew. She was a hair stylist who did Mike's hair every two or three weeks when he was in need of a haircut. Mike also helped this male friend in drugs, who would buy capsules through the mail and then divide and resell them. Mike helped in separating the capsules.

Further investigations revealed that Mike knew various other people who were into drugs. It was not determined whether his girl friend was into the drug scene, although she knew the circle of drug people and dated some guys Mike knew. The circle of drug people would not open their mouths. They were tight lipped. Therefore no leads were obtained.

Hoover checked the background of one of Mike's friends, the one with the hair stylist girl friend. He had an extensive criminal history. He was in jail on a drug bust when Mike and his girl friend disappeared, however. Later, he killed his hair stylist girl friend and he got away with it. They were in a love-hate relationship. One time, during their domestic violence eruption, she was sitting in a chair. He picked up his revolver and shot a hole in the chair just above her head. That was enough for her. She left him and went back home to her parents. They worked days. One day he came bouncing over on his motorcycle and made her take a ride with him. At high speed, he laid the motorcycle down, killing her. Hoover contacted her parents to obtain any information on Mike and his friends. They wouldn't say a word. They were very scared.

Mike's girl friend's mother had a daughter. Neither woman would furnish any information to Hoover. They had their minds made up about Mike's guilt. He's the guilty party, nothing further to be said. There could have been a jealous streak at one time between the mother and her daughter over Mike. There was an indication there might have been an affair between Mike and the mother at one point. However, the mother was very bitter and a very angry person. She wanted Mike caught and punished. She just knew Mike had killed her one daughter. The Lewis County detective believed her totally and so did the Pierce County detective. So their investigation's focus was only on Mike. They didn't want to look to any other possible avenues. So the killer's game plan worked out in their favor. They killed Mike and his girl friend without getting caught. They even moved their crime scene from one county to the other (Pierce to Lewis County).

The local television news media and a mystery program played up the theory that Mike was the likely killer and was hiding somewhere. The case ended up on the "Unsolved Mysteries." The detectives focused on Mike and assured viewers he'd be found. In later broadcasts, their stories began to change. They thought Mike might be dead. His best friend was interviewed and said he didn't know what happened but he also then thought Mike was dead. The detectives, however, did not undo their focus. Mike remained their target.

In early 1986, the police kept an all points bulletin out for Mike. There were no findings of him, just false reports. Investigator Hoover tried to do more, looking into the profile of his best friend. He had been Hoover's suspect since day one. He had knowledge of trapping, knew the trap lines, and he knew Mike's and his girl friend's movements. He was in with a circle of drug-related friends who would not talk.

There was a strange incident before Mike and his girl friend disappeared. Mike came home to his dad's house one evening. He placed a string outside to create an alarm that if tripped, would alert him in his room. The niece across from them noted a pickup truck pull up towards the house soon after Mike got home. It appeared they had been tailing Mike. Hoover obtained a general description of the truck, a 1988 Ford dark green pickup truck. It had been observed one time at the Sumner tavern where Mike hung out. Two brothers who owned the truck were into drugs. Hoover began surveillance on the truck. It revealed they hung out at the Sumner tavern and were dealing drugs. They had connections with other drug people including Mike's best friends. It was undetermined if there were any ties between the two brother's drug dealings. One brother died in a suicide involving drugs. He was deeply involved in drugs.

Hoover contacted a police psychic back East, and sent him one of Mike's belongings. The psychic's conclusion was that Mike's best friend was involved and knew who did the killings, but did not do the killings himself. That coincided with Hoover's theory all along. Mike's friend was always his number one suspect. He was the one who led the searches on the ground and in the air for the Pierce County Sheriff's Department.

Hoover's leads came to an end, except for Mike's best friend and his drug contacts. His theory was conclusive as follows:

Who: person or persons knowing both of the subjects

What: purpose was jealousy, revenge, or knowledge they had on drug dealing

84

When: planned by persons knowing the subjects, perfect time executed

Where: en route apprehension as they proceeded from trap line

Why: to eliminate Mike, possibly out of jealousy or a drug revenge hit or to keep Mike from revealing drug crime information to authorities

It all makes sense in theory, and it fits the profile.

On the basis of the private investigation, Hoover concluded the following. Mike's best friend had complete knowledge of the trap lines. He knew the time element – where he would be at a particular time en route or at the trap sights. People knew both of the subjects' stormy relationship back and forth. Yet on this particular winter day in December, the two got together and had their daughter with them. They left Mike's father's home in his pickup truck. There were domestic charges pending on Mike for the following week, but that didn't bother his girl friend. The plan to kill was in motion. Several males in pursuit of Mike's truck, driving their truck, also looked like trappers, but were indeed out to kill. We were sure these guys knew Mike and his girl friend. They may have not expected the girl friend and their daughter would be with him at that time. However, they were. Mike finished a big part of his trap line and had a pretty good catch that would deliver him a good sum of cash.

Mike and his girl friend apparently had a scheduled appointment to meet a blond woman at the Spanaway K-Mart. They met the blond, and the two women went into the store. Mike remained in his truck or may have gone over to the adjacent restaurant and lounge. In the distance, the men in the other truck appeared to be watching the whole thing. The blond left in her vehicle going northbound. Mike's girl friend met Mike at his truck. They headed south and apparently took a cut off to Yelm. The other truck followed in pursuit. There was finally a confrontation and the apprehended the trio. Mike possibly wasn't too alarmed and was off guard since he knew them. So they got the drop on them. It is possible Mike had damaging information on a crime linked to drugs.

After being apprehended, the two men took them for a ride into a deep wooded area. They placed Mike in the back of the truck. When they stopped, Mike's girl friend jumped out and began running with her daughter. They fell down and were caught. At this point, they took the minor child back to the K-Mart store, dropped her off, and left for Yelm and to the Bald Hill Road. There appeared to be two in the front seat of Mike's truck. On 1000 Line by Alder Lake, they killed Mike, possibly putting his body in a shallow grave. They kept Mike's girl friend and took her joy riding, sexually molesting and raping her periodically. They finally went to the secluded logging road off Highway 7 towards Morton. They drove the truck to the very end. There, they decided this was it for her. They had a little fun with her. They took her clothing off, did some perverted things, and finally stabbed her with Mike's knife. They bound her hands and the tube sock was placed around her neck. They went to their truck and left. It was cold and snowing. They knew that Mike would not be found, that he'd be the prime suspect, and that the police would not look any further. They were right.

Hoover's prime suspect has all the answers that have not been answered in this case. The police would not move on with it and Hoover could not make his case without hard evidence.

Mike's father, the retired game warden, passed on knowing in his heart that his son is dead and that the murderers got away with the perfect murders. At his funeral, the police showed up hoping Mike would be there.

This case remains open and an unsolved mystery.

The Hoover Agency has handled a variety of missing person cases, such as parental kidnappings of children raised by single parents in today's times. One out of five children under 18 are kidnapped by the other parent. Some end up in foreign lands. Current laws make it a felony, but this does not stop them all. The children themselves are really the victims, and nobody really wins. Missing person cases can end up with a homicide. Runaways can voluntarily return to their homes if not involved with drugs and the parents have the welcome mat out with lots of love, affections, communication, and understanding between parent and child. If a child stays on the streets, they can become hardened criminals. These are the throw-aways, children who are literally told to get out and stay out. Kidnappings can fall under many headings: parental, child porno, prostitution, black-market adoptions, psychotic murders, planned murder, or a hostage situation. A kidnapping is a trauma situation for a child. Like in custody cases, you need to know the complete situation about what is going on.

Domestic or divorce child-custody cases can end up in murder. The parent must be a fit person to obtain custody. Investigators must watch, observe, and analyze these cases to the fullest extent. Any parent going for custody must be reliable and competent. The primary concern is for the health and welfare of the child or children. Much love and understanding is needed when a divorce occurs. An investigator needs to prove a parent is unfit. Behaviors that can furnish that proof can include neglect, physical/emotional abuse, drugs/alcohol, molesting, living with many persons, continually moving, unstable home life, numerous marriages/separations, disharmony, cohabiting, sex, emotional abuse, yelling, and screaming. Children's behavior can also tip off investigators to poor home life and poor school grades or juvenile legal problems.

Missing person cases fall under many headings, as stated. Kidnappings, divorce, and custody issues can bring forth pressure that leads to emotional stress, and one could snap and you have a murder case on your hands. A local example is the Brame case in Tacoma where there was pressure from a domestic case and pending divorce, use of abusive measures, the power and corruption of the Tacoma chief of police, all of which led to the murder of the wife and the chief's suicide. Drugs and alcohol are other factors in murder/ suicides.

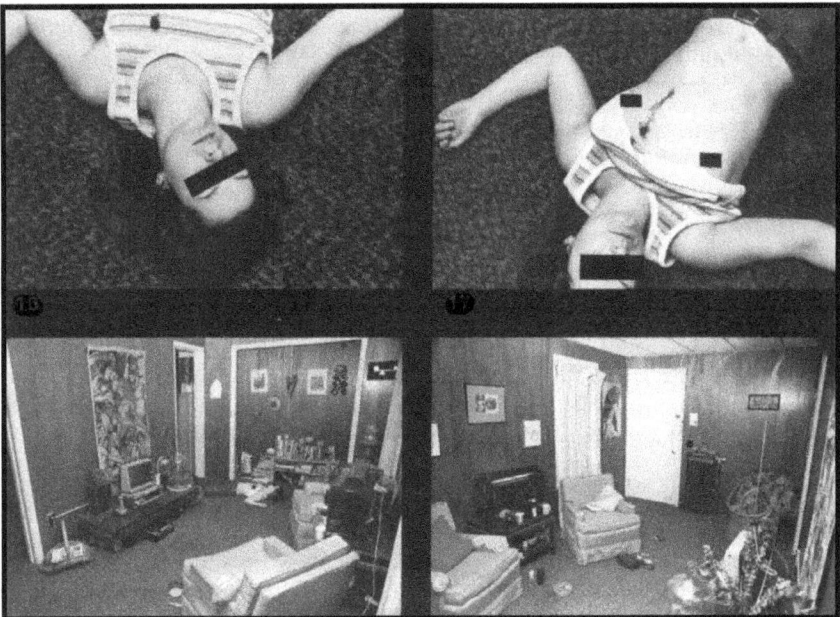

Homicide "crime scene photography"

Real Estate Homicide Case

Investigator Hoover was summoned to investigate the murder of a young, bright, attractive, California-raised woman. She moved to the great Northwest and lived in Lake Tapps with her boyfriend. She obtained her real estate license and was selling homes.

The 22-year old was a real go-getter. She located houses that needed to be sold. She made contact with owners, listed their houses, and ended up selling them. One afternoon she obtained a lead on a house that needed to be sold. She made contact with the owner. She made an appointment for that same evening.

She arrived on time, parked her car, and met the owner of the home. He invited her in and began showing her the home. Unknown to her, he was married. He and his wife were separating and in the process of a divorce. They planned on selling the home and splitting the equity. The owner was in the home alone and had been drinking alcohol quite heavily. When the woman arrived, he was feeling no pain. However, he was very much stressed out over the marital problems. Hoover gathered this information during the investigation process.

He gathered further intelligence on the owner by canvassing the neighborhood and interviewing neighbors. He learned that the couple was very nice and were good neighbors with no problems. However, during the past year, the husband had become very violent. His behavior problems were the result of drinking alcohol heavily and using prescription drugs. The combination turned the man into a monster.

The couple had no children. In one police incident report, the spouse called in a domestic violence situation. They were fighting with one another. The husband pulled out a 22-caliber automatic gun, grabbed her around the neck in a choke hold, and brought the gun up to her temple. He moved it so the barrel was just behind her ear. As he held her in a headlock, he pulled back the slide and clicked it into firing position. He then said, "I ought to blow your brains out." He then turned her loose. She ran and left the home. She went to the police station to make her report.

Hoover had a theory as to how the young real estate woman became a murder victim. She walked into a home with no idea what might happen of the circumstances involved with this couple. She stepped into a tiger's den. The husband had been home alone drinking alcohol heavily and popping pills. As he showed her the house, he started making heavy advances on her. She refused them. He became more angry and then violent. He became very physical, grabbing her and attempting to throw her down. She fought back and resisted in every manner. He came up with the 22 gun and forced her to submit. He now had control of the situation. When he finished having sex with her, he made her dress, get into her Ford pickup truck, and drive away with him. She was now a hostage in her own truck. He made her drive to a secluded area.

He made her stop the truck and attempted to have sex with her again. She fought him. She was not cooperating to his liking, so he began to be violent and lost his cool. He grabbed her around the neck, placed her in a headlock, placed the gun behind her ear, and pulled the trigger, killing her instantly. He pushed her over in the truck seat. He drove the vehicle back out onto the main highway and went due west. It was now very dark and the rain was pouring down heavily. The highway traffic was fairly heavy. Approaching the Orting exit, he pulled to the side of the road. He moved the vehicle under the bridge, parking it there. When the coast was clear, he exited the truck, leaving her body on the seat. He walked in the pouring rain up the hill to the Orting highway and walked to his girl friend's residence. A state patrol man passed the Ford truck several times that night but didn't stop to check it. The weather was windy and it was raining cats and dogs.

The following morning, the real estate office and her live-in boy friend were worried and had already called the police. Her boy friend decided to go out on his own to see if he could find her. He got into his truck and drove around. A number of hours later, he happened to see her truck on the main highway under the overpass bridge. He drove up behind and parked. He walked to her truck and opened the door. He was shocked and terrified about what he found. She was dead in the truck seat, just laying there lifeless with dried blood from her ear streaming down onto the seat. He ran as fast as he could and summoned the police. An investigation began and police arrested the home owner on murder charges. Hoover's investigation, as written above, also showed the home owner to be the main suspect and had done the crime.

Police and Hoover conducted a search in an attempt to find the murder weapon. Hoover's investigation concluded that the home owner had thrown the gun in the garbage, which was taken to the local dump.

Police were notified and a search of the dump site was not successful. The private investigation focused on proving his innocence or guilt. In court, he pleaded not guilty and said the real estate woman left his house in her truck. There were no eye witnesses in the neighborhood nor anywhere on the roads that the truck traveled. The home owner claimed that as soon as she left his house, he began walking to his girlfriend's house. He said he hitched a ride on the main highway and was dropped off at the Orting overpass bridge near her house. An alibi search was conducted to test his story. Hoover even advertised in the newspaper for the person who picked him up to come forward and collect a reward. Nobody responded. Hoover compared the mileage and time from the owner's house to his girlfriend's house with the time the owner said it took him to make that trip, and concluded that the man was lying. It did not pan out for him to be innocent.

At the man's trial, the prosecutor went for first degree murder based on evidence from the police investigation. The defense attorney claimed his client was under stress from the divorce and was medicated and under the influence of alcohol and therefore was not in his right state of mind. He claimed the defendant was not in his right mind. The jury found him guilty of manslaughter, a reduced charge. Case closed.

Note to realtors: Realtors are currently being targeted, stalked, robbed, raped, and murdered. To prevent that, go in pairs, observe your surroundings, and know your clients.

Monte Hoover
Associate Broker
503-645-7433 Ext. 223

Cell: 503-380-4365
Fax: 503-645-3049
Email: montehoover@johnlscott.com
Address: Sunset Corridor Office
1800 NW 167th Place Suite 100
Beaverton, OR 97006

www.JohnLScott.com

John L. Scott
REAL ESTATE

Oldest son

State Counselor Accused as Child Molester

Mel Hoover was called upon to help in the defense of a Tacoma half-way house counselor. Married with one child, he had been a professional counselor for a number of years. He worked with teenagers with problems, such as drug or alcohol abuse, prostitution, runaways, abused, and teens with mixed race families.

One day a week, the counselors took the group of boys and girls to a local apartment complex where they had use of the heated pool and recreational area. There was a balcony overlooking the pool from where their activities were observed. Usually, a counselor would also get into the pool with the children.

One day, Hoover's client said, he supervised the children on the outing, every step of the way from leaving the half-way house until they returned. He said he had continuous problems with two females, ages 13 and 15. They smoked marijuana and disobeyed counselors and the half-way house rules. The counselor said he came down hard on the girls because of their behavior, taking away various privileges and placing them on restriction. He wanted them to straighten up and make a difference with their life styles, to learn what's right and what's wrong. However their behavior and attitudes did not change. They kept challenging him and continued to cause problems. Apparently counselors more or less let them break a lot of rules, allowing a number of offenses go over their heads, uncaring about their future.

On this particular day, the counselor entered the pool with the teens and gave swimming pointers to some of the children. The 15-year-old got out of the pool and sat across the pool on its edge and watched. Everyone was having a good time, splashing about. Then the 13-year-old swam over close to the counselor with a big grin on her face. Then it was time for everyone to get out of the pool. Everyone dressed, was escorted to the bus, and rode back to the half-way-house.

Without the counselor's knowledge, the two girls made a formal complaint with two other supervisors against Hoover's client. Other counselors said they had seen Hoover's client in the pool with the girls, but did not see any inappropriate activities. The compliant stated that when the girl was next to the counselor in the pool, that he took hold of her, fondled her breast, and then stuck his finger into her vagina. She said she swam away and exited the pool.

91

The staff called Child Protective Services but did not talk to the accused counselor or perform any investigation of their own. They believed the story to be true. The police were called, a report made, and the prosecutor filed charges against the counselor and arrested him at the half-way house. He went to jail but was released on bail. He hired an attorney who asked Hoover to investigate.

Hoover obtained the police report, interviewed the counselor, and began the investigation. He went to the swimming pool and looked at the balcony overlooking the pool. He photographed the empty pool from all directions and from the balcony. He returned when the pool was in use and re-photographed the pool. He observed that when the pool was not in use, he could see the bottom. But when people were in the pool, he could not see the bottom nor any portion of the people's bodies under the water. It was just all one great blur, even from across the pool where the older girl said she had observed the incident. It was evident the two girls were lying about the incident.

The investigator canvassed the pool for any witnesses to the incident. He did not locate any. He went back again on the same day and hour that the incident occurred and re-canvassed for witnesses. He was about to call it quits when he noticed a well dressed woman on the balcony. He approached her, identified himself, and explained why he was there. She said she was on the pool's balcony the day of the incident and at the time of the incident. She re-membered observing the pool and noting everyone in the pool was enjoying themselves. She said the water was a complete blur with waves and splashing, and she could only see the upper parts of swimmers' bodies. As the witness worked at the state capitol building in Olympia and appeared to be a reliable witness, Hoover obtained a written statement from her.

The investigator ran a background check on each of the individuals involved in the incident. Both the teenage girls had a history of running away, using drugs, rude behavior, disregard for rules and instructions. Both were habitual liars. The 13-year-old liked her sex and had run away for sexual activities repeatedly. Just a week before the incident, she ran away one evening and was found in an abandoned garage having sex with a teenage male. She was taken back to the half-way house and released to the counselor. Police made their report, as did the counselors, and placed them in their file records.

Hoover submitted his report to the attorney the following day, just a couple days before the case was ready to go to court.

Hoover then contacted the police officer who had found the teen having sex in the garage. The officer confirmed the information in the report. Hoover forwarded that information to the attorney.

The next day, the attorney contacted the prosecuting attorney and presented his case to him. The prosecutor decided to drop the charges providing a release was signed promising that no civil law suits would be pursued against the half-way house and the counselors or the police officers, the department, or the city of Tacoma. The attorney's client agreed, and the case was dismissed. Case closed.

Note: The client's career was ruined and he almost lost his wife and child from threatened divorce proceedings. As the case was closed with no charges, he regained a new career and his marriage was saved.

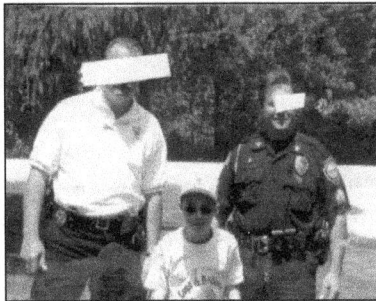

Apprehended, boy, sex with minor female

Police motorcycle patrol division

Northwest Racketeering Cases

Racketeering cases involved people within the Pierce County Sheriff's Department, including the sheriff. Bail bondsmen and a car lot owned by the owner of a bail bond company were also involved. The used car lot was operated by the bondsman's son. That mob grew in size but eventually 12 of the 15 or more were busted and jailed. Others involved agreed to testify in federal court and were let go. Innocent police officers were being blamed for various acts to help the mob, but those accusations were neither true nor proven.

The Hoover Investigation agency ran across suspicious circumstances in a few night clubs and strip joints through the years where prostitution and illegal gambling were occurring and appeared to be protected by the sheriff's department. The agency made periodic reports to the department, but nothing changed.

In 1977, the department was plagued by racketeering. Things began to snowball. There was a smell in the air that the sheriff was dirty. He was liked by all the officers and detectives in the department. He had been an officer who had risen through the ranks to become sheriff. Many were aware what was going on, especially the sheriff's activities, but they were overlooked.

Hoover grew up in the era when there was a known mob presence in the area. The Carbone family had used car lots. Carbone also owned a large bail bond business in Tacoma. For years, the mob controlled certain taverns and topless dance clubs and was involved with a variety of criminal activities. It had been going on for a long time. Racketeering was not new in Tacoma, but it was well hidden from most people. Then later, they got the sheriff hooked into their criminal activities.

One day, a member of the kingpin's family called Hoover to provide protection services. They were deeply concerned about domestic violence between the kingpin's son and daughter-in-law. Young children were involved. The wife and her family were afraid for their lives and those of the children because death threats had been made. The son operated his father's used car lots and was tied in deeply with the mob. One night, he went into a rage, went home, broke down the door, and assaulted his wife and children. He said he'd be back to kill them all, including any of her family members who got involved.

Norwest Mob

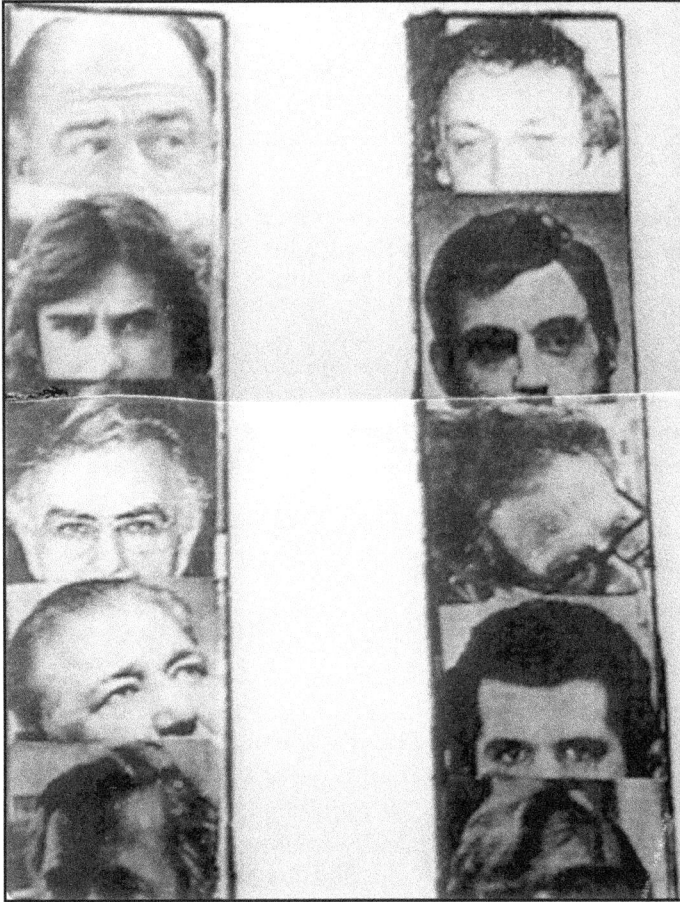

Some of the people in the Northwest racketeering case involving people within the Pierce County Sheriff Department. Primary perpetrators were the sheriff and a bail bondsman, who also owned a used car lot. His son operated the car lot. Their mob grew in numbers and was eventually busted. 12 of the 15 were jailed and the others agreed to testify at the federal court trial. The trial proved that innocent police officers were being blamed for acts committed by the mob.

He said he'd take them out if they got in his way. He was under pressure from his dad and the mob activities, so he snapped and began taking it out on his family.

Hoover and his investigators put a plan into action where two armed investigators would guard inside the house, watching all the windows and doors. They used walkie talkies to stay in contact with other investigators patrolling in vehicles and on foot outside the house. Upon any sign of suspicious activity around the home, all the investigators would communicate by radio and would be alert and ready. The mother and children were placed in a safe room inside the house with an investigator close by.

Throughout the night, everyone was on edge knowing that the husband could use any of his henchmen and any of his used cars to strike. Around midnight, a couple vehicles appeared in the area, but they were false alarms.

When morning came, the mother and children were quickly escorted to a vehicle carrying small suitcases. They were moved quickly out of the area. Hoover placed a vehicle in front of and behind the mother and children's car for protection. They took an alternate route from there to one of her relative's home, where they were released to her family, and they all disappeared out of town where the husband, Joey, was unable to find them.

Meanwhile, another problem arose for the mob. They had problems with a liquor inspector who kept hounding them at some of their taverns and topless clubs. Throughout the years, city and county police had made several reports of possible criminal activities in those establishments, but the report seemed to disappear and no investigations were ever enacted. The average police officer was really unaware of what was going on. Some had an idea but let is slide on by. The bad officers were basically working for the sheriff. The good officers just went along with the flow, more or less closing their eyes to the whole thing.

The mob felt very secure with the sheriff in their pocket and a few officers backing him. The bail bond business was booming, making the kingpin money hand over fist. He always seemed to have a bondsman at the jail. There were about 10 mobsters in the gang including the sheriff. But the liquor inspector was a thorn in their side. So they decided to schedule a hit. They hired two inexperienced hoods to assassinate the inspector and planned a malicious smear campaign before and after he was to be gunned down to draw attention away from them.

When the hoods shot into the liquor inspector's vehicle, but he immediately laid down. He was hit by gunfire, but survived. He recovered from his wounds, but the cloud of rumors the mob had started haunted him. They claimed that he took bribes and engaged in illicit love affairs. The mob also attacked their competitors by hiring arsonists to burn them out. They hoped to throw off suspicion from their gangster mob. The chief liquor inspector underwent a polygraph test that absolved him from any wrong doing. With the can of worms now opened, the state and FBI began an investigation.

Hoover had known of the illegal activities these people had been doing for years. He reported it again, but it was pushed under the rug again. During one of Hoover's investigations, a night club stripper and one of her girl friends appeared with knowledge of the criminal activities going on in the clubs. Both women had been involved in prostitution. Her girl friend was heavily into drugs. But because of all the investigations, club employees began to feel uneasy. The stripper quit out of the blue. When she had her son with her during a visitation period, she took off with him, escorted with transportation by her boyfriend.

The young boy's father, who was Hoover's client, wanted Hoover to track his son down. Hoover determined his mother had left for Kansas with her boyfriend. The boy's mother went to her mother's home. Hoover located the address for the client. The client had legal custody but was financially unable to pursue the investigation any further. On Hoover's recommendation, he flew out there to get his son back. He got lucky. He saw his son outside playing and snapped him up and sped back to the airport with him and took him home, safe and sound.

The other girl friend in Tacoma mentioned she had knowledge of, and kept notes of, the man's activities and reported them to the sheriff several times. But her notes disappeared. Later, authorities who wanted her for a witness tried to contact her but found her overdosed on heroin. It was, in fact, a homicide, a convenient cover-up for the mob. Even one of the clubs' doormen and bouncer was taken for a ride. He knew too much and was shot in his car and dumped into Wapato Lake where his body was found a week later. During another homicide at Point Defiance Park, a car and driver ran off an embankment. Many of these murders during this period, were unsolved.

When the state's and FBI's investigations were complete, arrests were made one by one. A few individuals turned state's evidence and went into the witness protection program. The kingpin received a 100-year prison sentence. His son, Joey, received an 18-year sentence. The rest received 10-12-year sentences. In the end, there were 15 in the mob, including the sheriff. All were convicted and sent to prison.

These cases prove that corruption can be anywhere in government, from the top down to small departments. There are the good, the bad, and the ugly in all professions. While all that crime and corruption came to a head in that century, who's saying it won't occur in the next century too? It has continued in high scam operations involving well-known corporations involved in stock investments, in energy firms, and back into local police departments, such as the 2003 Tacoma domestic case of Chief Brame. Corruption will probably continue on into the next century.

Getting back to the old racketeering case, a special prosecutor was assigned to investigate all persons associated with the organized crime figures. Charges were filed against the Pierce County jailers for receiving gifts in exchange for referring prisoners to the kingpin's bail bondsmen.

A number of charges were brought against a number of officers. The court appointed Hoover's agency to investigate the allegations and provide reports for the jailers' defense attorney. He obtained information from a variety of witnesses, including the jailers, people who had been arrested, and other officers. The special prosecutor was claiming it was a conspiracy among the jailers and city and county police officers to refer prisoners to the kingpin's bail bond company. When prisoners were booked into jail, they would ask, "Where can I get a bail bondsman quickly?" The jailer would offer the telephone book and say that there was a bail bondsman standing out in the hall the prisoner could use. Since the person wanted to get out of jail as quickly as possible, they would usually pick the agent in the hall. The company made sure one was there day or night. In return, the company left gifts for the jailers in their lockers or cars. They in turn would say they did not know where the gifts came from or who to return them to, but in fact they did have some idea or know. That did not make them guilty.

Hoover gathered affidavits and documents for each of the jailer defendants. Upon receiving the reports, the defense attorneys went head to head with the special prosecutor. Once the attorneys provided their facts, the prosecutor dropped all charges. Case closed.

The Art Theft

Mel Hoover, PI, in May, the month of his birthday, received several drawings from two of his daughters. Then the telephone rang. It was a person who dealt in old art work: paintings and antiques in general. Though his daughter's gifts did not fall into that category, the theft of art and antiques was the subject of their phone conversation. Hoover was hired for another case by a new client.

Hoover went to Lakewood and to an expensive, modern home on Lake Steilacoom. A middle-aged woman invited him into her home. She was fairly good looking and wore a very expensive dress and jewelry. She was fit to be tied. She described a theft of two valuable oil canvas paintings signed by a well known artist. Also stolen were two statues by a well known sculptor and a collectable lamp, both also marked.

Hoover reviewed the police report and inspected the home's built-in alarm system. He discovered the thieves had bypassed the alarm and entered the home knowing exactly what they wanted and took them. It appeared as though it was an inside job. There were no signs of breaking and entering, and no finger prints were found. No one had observed a suspicious vehicle about the premises.

The investigator determined that someone had made an impression of a rear door key and had used it to enter the home. The goods were carried to an adjacent bushy area where they apparently had a truck waiting. They quickly left the scene of the crime.

Investigator Hoover compiled a list of everyone associated with the home. There were a maid, butler, various friends, and a maintenance and yard man. They were all considered suspects. He gathered background information on them all, a process that ended up with one prime suspect: the maintenance man. His background showed that he was art oriented, and his finances were in bad shape. Hoover found out he did have some very expensive art paintings and artifacts that had recently been sold to an art and antique dealer who was known to fence stolen paintings and antiques. He dealt with middle men who had overseas contacts. It was an illegal business that auctioned off art and antiques for a hefty sum of money.

Surveillance began, and the police were made aware of the situation and cooperated with the investigation. Hoover zoomed in on his suspect. Apparently, the suspect felt the pressure or may have

Art thefts are a reality. Two of Hoover's three lovely daughters used their artistic skills to draw two pictures for their old dad on his 50th birthday. They presented them to dad using the phrase, "We detected a birthday, dad!"

Old dad, Mel Hoover Jr., turned 72 writing this book. His daughter, Jennie Kissinger, shown with her drawing, for Dad.

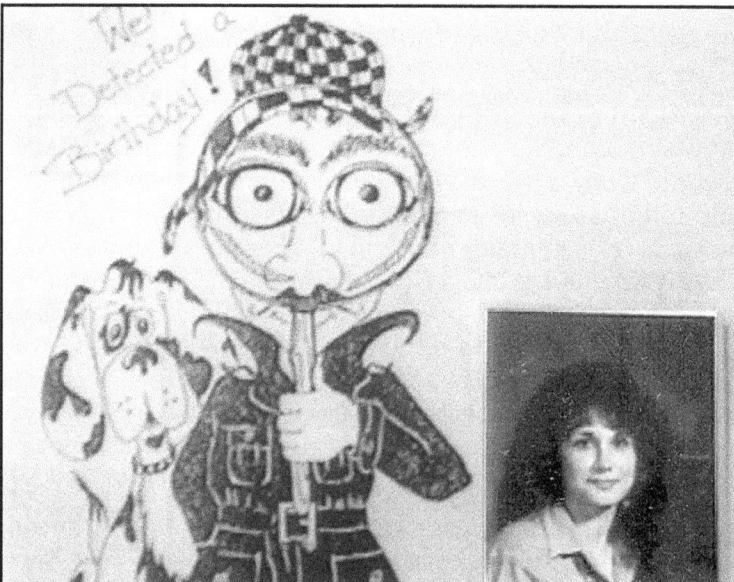

obtained information that they were on to him. The heat became too much for him. Hoover soon received a call from his client. She reported that she had left her home and returned. She was very excited and shouted, "My oil art paintings and antiques have returned. They're all sitting in the center of my living room. Thank you! Thank you!"

The client updated her alarm system with video cameras and better door and window locks. The maintenance man was fired and was still under police investigation when the case was closed.

Book of Living Artists 13th;
ArtNetwork Press; Drawing by–

Drawing contest of "DJ" and Shandra during their tender years by Jennie

Aviation Accident Investigation

A California investigator, who covered Washington, Oregon, and California for an aircraft company, contacted PI Hoover to assist in an investigation of a crash of a twin-engine Beechcraft airplane. The two investigators met, put their heads together, and began investigating the crash near McChord AFB outside of Tacoma.

They canvassed the crash site extensively and interviewed many witnesses. They obtained statements and affidavits regarding the crash. They learned that the night of the crash was very dark and stormy. Lightning was flashing around a small, self-sufficient Tacoma airport a few miles across the Tacoma Narrows Bridge and Puget Sound. The airport had nicely laid-out runways and a tower that many small planes utilized. The Beechcraft left the loading area there that night, taxied out onto the runway, and was given clearance for takeoff by the tower. The plane lifted off and climbed upward. After reaching its proper altitude, it leveled off and began a scheduled flight South to Bakersfield, California and then to Las Vegas, Nevada.

The radar screens showed the aircraft approached McChord and headed south. The next thing the airport and McChord towers heard was a mayday cry over the radio. The plane quickly disappeared from the radar screens after the distress call. It crashed several miles south of McChord AFB in a wooded area with an open clearing. There were five people aboard, all in their early twenties. Observers on the ground heard the troubled plane. They looked up and saw it in a very steep dive straight down at a high rate of speed. The wings flew off before the fuselage spiraled down, crashing into the ground and killing all onboard.

Investigators salvaged every piece of the aircraft. There were many parts and pieces. It was all gathered up to be analyzed and inspected to put the puzzle into perspective. It was all classified as evidence in the case. Many volunteers were used to gather the pieces, including the Boy Scouts of America and the Air Force Search and Rescue Team. . The Federal Aviation Agency investigates every crash scene. The FAA and the two private investigators oversaw the search.

A background investigation began on the young pilot in question. It was learned that he was inexperienced. He had held a private pilot's license for less than one year. Witnesses' statements confirmed that the small plane was overloaded. One potential passenger had even backed out of the flight when he noticed the overloading.

The pilot's parents began a lawsuit against the aircraft company. They claimed the manufacturer was negligent for faulty construction of the plane. They claimed that the wing bolts were highly corroded which resulted in the wings separating from the aircraft body.

Witnesses who had observed the plane in flight noted the very stormy conditions that included heavy rain, wind, and lightning. They said they could not believe there was a plane up there flying in those conditions. The ground crew at the airport had observed the overloading and had advised the pilot. Yet he took off anyway. Witnesses near the crash scene said they heard and saw the aircraft flying. They could hear the aircraft's engines in a high-pitched roar. They saw the plane in a steep dive. The wings came off, and then there was a thud after the dive. Smoke filled the air in the distance.

The Beechcraft Company had all the pieces of the wings possible and every linking piece. They put the puzzle together regarding the wing bolts. They brought in technicians to obtain evidence to defend the company and its reputation. They included structural engineers, aeronautical engineers, and metallurgical corrosion engineers. They sent the wing bolts to a lab for testing of corrosion and strength.

The court trial began in the Pierce County Courthouse in Tacoma. It lasted a week as experts testified for both sides. The investigators' witnesses testified to what they saw and heard. The airport ground crew said they advised the pilot not to take off in the bad weather with the overloading condition. The pilot's background was presented, documenting his inexperience to fly in the bad weather conditions.

The jury weighed the evidence and found the pilot to have been negligent and responsible for the crash. No evidence proved the wing bolts were corroded or caused the crash. The case was won and closed.

The Drug Bust

One bright sunny spring day, Investigator Hoover was scheduled to perform surveillance on a house on the outskirts of Bremerton, Washington. The sun was reflecting off the inlet waterway. Surveillance began in the morning and he determined that a mother, a child, and the mother's male companion were inside. By afternoon, no sufficient activities were noted. Hoover was out of sight watching the front of the house while his partner was watching the east side and rear of the two-story house.

During the afternoon, however, Hoover saw two young adult males arrive at the house on foot. They entered the front door and within minutes were back outside looking around very hard and talking. They reached the sidewalk and turned east towards Hoover's partner. There was a grove of bushes on the corner where they stopped shortly and looked inside the bushes. They then observed a police patrol unit driving nearby, so they decided to walk away and down the sidewalk. After the patrol passed, they made a quick bee-line back to the bushes and picked up a package. One suspect placed the package under his coat. It appeared very suspicious to Hoover, who got on the two-way radio with his partner. Hoover decided to apprehend them. The two investigators proceeded towards the two males who were walking toward the house.

The men saw the car bearing down on them with the other investigator on foot. They split up and started running in opposite directions. They ran at full bore in an outburst of speed as though in a dead-heat race. One suspect eluded Hoover's partner, but Hoover managed to hang with his subject who had the package under his coat. He ran very fast and far down the street and up another street. He kept zagging from street to street, over fences and through alleys. He attempted to hide on several occasions, but Hoover spotted him. So he moved onward, running hard. He became exhausted, and when he tried running up another street, he finally stopped as Hoover drove up along side of him. He was out of breath and very tired. He said, "You have nothing on me."

Hoover frisked him, hand-cuffed him, and pulled out the hidden package. It contained a brick of marijuana.

Hoover's partner called the police. Hoover met up with his partner as the police patrol unit pulled up. They exchanged information and took Hoover's suspect into custody. As another police unit arrived on the scene, they observed a young male hiding in the nearby bushes. They apprehended him and put him in the patrol car. The two were arrested on drug possession charges.

Investigators gave police further information that these young adults came from the house they were watching. That gave police probable cause for a warrant. Later, the house was raided and drugs were found inside. The young woman was arrested and her minor child was placed in custody of the father. Case closed.

Police patrol car

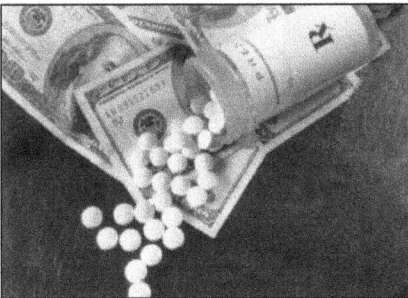

Prescription drug abuse in America, estimated at 25 to 30% of the population, is a big problem

The Child Snatch

During the early summer, Hoover received a call from an agency in New York. They told Mel that their client's spouse had run away with a young son, and that they had found her in Tacoma. The agency wanted Hoover to confirm that she was in Tacoma. Hoover learned that the father had legal, temporary custody of the child. Hoover obtained the mother's name, date of birth, social security number, and her last known address.

Hoover checked at that address, but the woman had moved. He learned of the current address and began surveillance there for a couple days to confirm the woman was living there with her son. He called the New York agency and gave a verbal report on the circumstances where she was and her movements about the community. They replied that they were flying out to Tacoma to snatch the child and return him to his father, their client. So two private investigators took the next flight to Seattle-Tacoma International Airport. They contacted Hoover and discussed using a van to continue surveillance.

They began surveillance on the house in the morning. After hours passed, they noted no activity. They knocked on the front door. The woman answered the door with her son behind her in a stroller. The investigator used a pretext, asking about the previous renter by name, having already done his homework and knowing the tenant's name. No suspicion was aroused. The investigator left and returned to the van. He said the woman was putting on a coat, and it appeared that she was about to leave her house. Surveillance continued.

The woman and child in the stroller came out of the house about ten minutes later. She walked away from the house to the main street. She turned east toward a small shopping area. They observed the child as he was being pushed down the sidewalk. The van moved slowly up the street, pulling off onto a side street past the woman. The two New York investigators quickly exited the van. One detained the mother while the other snatched the stroller and child from her. She began yelling and screaming for help, crying. The investigators ran and disappeared from her view. They quickly got into the van and sped off down the side street. The woman did not get a look at the van.

The van drove to a downtown Tacoma rental car lot. They exited the van and got into a rental car heading to the airport. They caught their scheduled flight and returned to New York. The Hoover Agency van quickly disappeared back to the Tacoma office.

The child was returned to the client. The mother would need to return to New York and take legal steps in an attempt to regain her custody. However, having left the state with her son would possibly hurt her case. Case closed.

"Terrorist" child snatch – SWAT team member of police department rescues the hostage child

Executive Protection Case

Investigator Hoover was called to meet a very prominent business woman. During the call, arrangements were made for the meeting at a secluded, back-wood restaurant near Mount Rainier National Park.

Hoover arrived prior to the time for the scheduled appointment. He parked his car on the side of the restaurant in order to see the parking lot plus the main highway. He sat waiting. Right on time, a new, white Mercedes coupe arrived and parked next to the restaurant. It was the business woman. She exited her car. She was very well dressed in a nice blouse and skirt, black high heeled shoes with a matching suit jacket. Her hair was red and neck length. Her height, weight, and body measurements matched her description to a T. She was attractive but professional looking. Her slender body moved with ease and her bosoms stood out and bounced as she walked into the restaurant.

In the corner of his eye, Hoover observed a vehicle in the distance. His gut instinct told him the vehicle had been following her. It stayed back, observing the restaurant. Hoover went inside, met her, and spoke briefly. She said she was in need of a bodyguard because she felt she was being stalked and her life might possibly be in danger. She said her business was losing business to her competitors and that intelligence about her business was being gathered by someone.

Hoover told her someone had possibly followed her to the restaurant. She hired Hoover on the spot. He told her to leave and that he would follow. She left in her car. The other vehicle pulled in behind her. As Hoover brought up the rear and was gaining on the second car, all of a sudden the black Mustang Cobra hit the throttle. Its tires smoked as it sped past his client, leaving Hoover in a smoke cloud and without having obtained the car's license number or description of the driver. Things were back to square one. Who was the stalker in question?

He met the client at her house. He checked out the house and the surrounding grounds. It was secure. He escorted her day and night to and from her house to work and other activities. She finally said it might be her ex-husband behind all this.

She was guarded day and night by investigator Hoover. One night, she came out of her bedroom and toward Hoover in a see-through negligee. He was amazed and his heart pounded as she tried to seduce him. He put her off in a very subtle way and said they needed to keep the relationship professional for now. She agreed. So he guarded her for about a month.

During that time, Hoover recommended further services. She once again agreed on countermeasures to debug the house and the business, looking for high-tech electronic transmitters (bugs, wire taps, hidden microphones). Hoover's agency did an electronic RF sweep and physical searches of rooms and phones at the house and business. Further searches were made for carrier current transmissions or infrared light plus audio and video camera invasions. Hoover discovered a tape recorder on the home and business phone lines. He made attempts to physically catch the subject, but failed. However he obtained fingerprints from the recorder. They matched her ex-husband's. Hoover provided that evidence to the client's attorney. The former husband was out to destroy her and her business.

Her attorney took proper legal action. No criminal charges were filed, but an out-of-court settlement was agreed upon. The ex-husband paid her a million dollars.

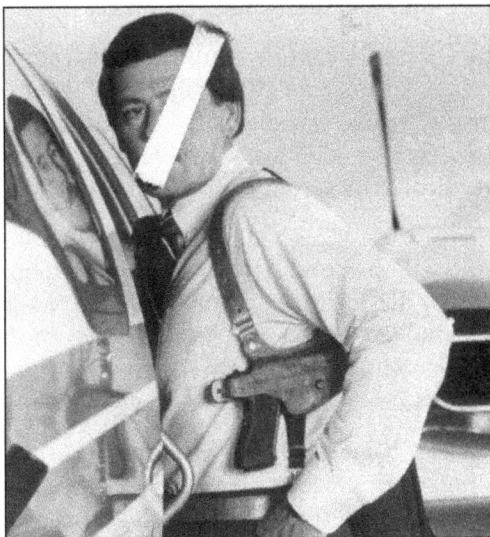

"Investigator" providing executive
protection for person flying out

Theft and Repossession Investigation

Mel Hoover received a phone call one day from a Midwest detective agency. They said they were working with an attorney regarding a civil theft, which boiled down to being just a repossession case.

They said a Midwest couple purchased a very expensive new 21-foot Bayliner boat with an inboard motor. They also bought a trailer for the boat. They made a down payment, and then moved out of the state, leaving no forwarding address. Nobody knew of their whereabouts. The detective agency had developed a lead after months of searching. They thought the couple was residing in the Bremerton, Washington, area. They had an address they asked Hoover to verify.

The couple was making itself very scarce, so Hoover found it difficult to track them down. However, a break came when a person remembered seeing them and their fancy boat while fishing in Silverdale, Washington. Hoover went to Silverdale. He looked around and contacted the sheriff there and explained the situation to him. He replied that he had not seen them around.

Hoover then found a local post office address for them and from there obtained a physical address in Silverdale. He went to the address and found a small, white, single-story, ranch-type house off the roadway way back in a wooded area. The long dirt drive way leading to the house was across the street from Hood Canal, a bay which lead to the Pacific Ocean.

Hoover observed the house and saw the trailer and boat parked next to it. He began surveillance of the house to learn the couple's habits, activities, and movements. After two days, he saw them take the boat and go fishing on Hood Canal. On the third day, the couple left the house without the boat.

Having already been referred to an Olympia attorney to learn the details on the repossession procedure, Hoover contacted the attorney again. He set into motion action to repossess the boat. A repossession truck and Hoover went onto the property. The truck loaded the trailer and boat and took it to an Olympia storage area provided by the attorney. Hoover waited for the couple to return home later that evening and served legal repossession papers on them. When the man answered the door, he and his wife were in shock, wondering what had happened to their boat. Their emotions appeared to be put on. Hoover left and contacted the attorney and provided an affidavit and investigation report to him. Criminal charges were filed against the couple, but they did not stick. It turned out to be just another white-collar crime that did not have the financial backing to pursue a successful prosecution. Does crime pay? Case closed.

Theft of Boat/Repossessed

Boat to the right is the target's boat out fishing in adjacent waterway

Injury Accident
Reconstruction Investigation

A local attorney representing a California law firm called Mel Hoover regarding a vehicle accident that occurred in Tacoma. A California couple purchased a new Jeep 4x4 pickup truck for their 20-year-old son. He and his 19-year-old passenger were both injured seriously in the accident. The son was transported from a Tacoma hospital to one in California for further treatment. It appeared the son could become a paraplegic, never to walk again. The parents wanted an investigation, which would consist of an accident reconstruction at the scene.

He began the investigation by studying the police report, canvassing the neighborhood, and interviewing people in the immediate area. There were no eye witnesses to the accident. Some people had heard the crash and went to the scene where they called police and an ambulance.

The accident occurred at 1 a.m. one summer when the sky was clear, the asphalt road dry, and little traffic was on the road. The Jeep was traveling westbound in the 2200 block of 72nd Street. The street was within the city limits. On the North side of the street was city property and on the South side of 72nd Street was Pierce County property. Since the Jeep was traveling Westbound, it was on the city side of the border. It crossed over the center line and hit a power pole on the county side of the street. The car was completely totaled. The issue of whether liability fell to the city or county was in question.

An accident reconstruction began with still photos being taken of the street, street signs, conditions, visibility from the driver's perspective, and the crash site. A video camera was mounted in a vehicle as it recreated the path the Jeep traveled. It showed the view the driver would have as it crested the hill while traveling over the 35-mile-per-hour speed limit and crossed over to the pole and crash site. Measurements were taken of the road and used to estimate the speed of the vehicle for impact analysis. Photos were taken of the pole and skid marks. Measurements were taken and diagrams drawn for analysis. Statements of police officers and ambulance teams at the scene were taken.

Photographs were taken of the car, inside, outside, top, underneath, from all sides and from various angles. A physical inspection of its tires, front-end members, tie rods, steering gear and steering wheel, and brakes was made. There was no indication of speed on impact on the speedometer or tachometer. The truck's manual transmission was in high gear.

The results of accident reconstruction revealed that as the Jeep traveled westward on 72nd Street, its speed was about 50 MPH, in excess of the 35 MPH speed limit. As it approached a slight hill, its visibility was limited. It crested over the hill, which had a 1% slope, and passed several intersecting streets. With the roller-coaster effect of cresting the hill, the driver lost control and crossed over the center line with the wheels turned to the left. He hit the brakes, locking them up. The vehicle slid to the left side, and then rotated counter clockwise at it hit the power pole. It wrapped itself around the pole mid-center of the car. The driver was thrown out of the driver's door and landed on the ground adjacent to the vehicle. The passenger side of the Jeep hit the pole, pinning the passenger inside the truck. The truck's cab literally separated from the truck bed. From the direct impact on the passenger's door, the truck bent in a 90-degree angle around the pole. The pole was damaged. The driver's door was open. Neither the driver nor passenger wore seat belts.

The street had good overhead lighting, the asphalt road was dry, and the temperature was 60 degrees. The road was straight running East-West. It was a four-lane road with two lanes going each direction. At the crest of the hill, the road became a bit wavy, giving cars a roller coaster effect. There was a speed sign specifying a 35 MPH limit.

No mechanical defects were found on the Jeep. The police had found a shotgun behind the truck's seat.

The police and hospital reports indicated that the driver's blood-alcohol level was .19. When photographing and inspecting the vehicle, investigators observed beer cans inside and at the scene. Photographs documented that evidence. Hoover's investigation determined that the couple had left a party in Puyallup and were headed to another one in Tacoma at the time of the crash.

Their friends were located and interviewed. They said the two left with the intention of crashing the Tacoma party. They said they had been drinking in Puyallup and were under the influence of alcohol when they left.

The conclusion of the investigation was that neither the vehicle's condition nor street conditions caused the accident. The cause, as indicated by the .19 blood alcohol level in the driver, was driving under the influence of alcohol without regard for the safety of others.

The legal action being considered by the California parents and their attorneys was dropped because the investigation revealed no other party's liability. Only the driver's negligence was proven to have caused the accident. Case closed.

Accident Information

(1)   Site Inspection / Draw Site

(2)   Photography Still/Video (vehicles)

(3)   History of Vehicles

(4)   Driver's Licenses and Driving Records

(5)   Employment Verification of All

(6)   Criminal-Civil Records Searches of All

(7)   Interview Ambulance Driver(s)

(8)   Interview Tow Truck Operator(s)

(9)   Interview Emergency Room Personnel / Records?

(10)   Autopsy and Toxicology Reports

(11)   Interview All Witnesses / Obtain Statements

(12)   Reconstruction of Accident / Impact

(13)   Inspect Seatbelts and Interior

(14)   Product Liability?

(15)   Modifications of Vehicle

(16)   Condition of Vehicle – Damages / Repair

(17)   Inspect Tires, Speedometer, etc.

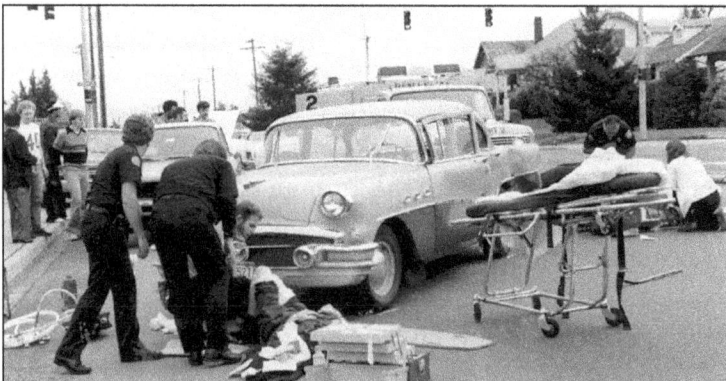

The Imposter Fraud Scammer

Investigator Hoover was call during the winter months by a middle aged woman who wanted a background investigation on a Caucasian male. He was very good looking, charming, and was a very smooth talker. He claimed he was a physician, but his identity was in question. He had a very common name.

The investigation began using his name, approximate date of birth, and locations. Nothing was found.

More identifiers were needed to prove or disprove his identity. Inquiries were made about his education at the University of Washington and Harborview Hospital. Nothing was available as he was unknown to them. So the investigation continued.

Hoover attempted to trace his address history by tracing his cell phone number. The address turned out not to be legitimate. He used the university credit cards to pay for hotel and motel stays, and then he would disappear. An address he used turned out to be a golf course in Richland, Washington. A check of the Drug Enforcement Administration about his authority to dispense narcotic drugs found that he was unregistered and unknown.

With so many unsubstantiated claims, he became a suspected imposter, a criminal in disguise. He was possibly a scammer involved in defrauding or other criminal activities.

Hoover met with his client and explained what he had learned. He explained he had nothing to prove or disprove his actions. The woman gave Hoover the license plate number of the vehicle the suspect was driving. Hoover checked the plate and it was incorrect. Apparently his client had gotten it all wrong.

She had originally met the suspect in eastern Washington. Her friends, who lived there and were hunting, met the man in a lounge and had dinner with him. They introduced him to Hoover's client. They went out, had dinner and a few drinks. When she left him, she went to her car in the parking lot. He watched as she backed out and struck another vehicle. She looked at the other car without getting out of her car, and seeing no damage, left.

The suspect continued courting her. He showered her with flowers, frequent calls, and visits to her home. One day he sprang a story on her. He said, "You know that car you hit in the parking lot? The owners called the police about the damage you did to it. I paid them $2,000."

The woman thought that was very nice of him, so she wrote him a check for $2,000. The check was returned with his name and a Montana driver's license, but it was not readable.

He kept courting her, and she became uneasy with his actions and behavior. She gave him $50 for gas one time just to get rid of him. Another time he said he needed to get his 48-foot Carver boat docked in Seattle, but his bank accounts were frozen while he tried to clear up the mess. Later, he returned to her home dressed to kill. He had x-rays which he showed to her. He said he was going to Iraq to perform surgery. Then he brought out a receipt for $3,800 for the car damage that she caused in Eastern Washington. He said he wanted to take care of it for her but his accounts hadn't been cleared up yet, so he needed $1,800. The client agreed to meet him at a lounge in a couple days to pay him. This time she obtained a correct Washington license plate number for his Ford Explorer.

Hoover ran the plate and it belonged to a man and wife in Eastern Washington. There was no indication the car was stolen. Hoover contacted the registered owner who said the car was stolen. They had reported the theft to police in Benton County, giving them the thief's name and date of birth. Police there said the man was wanted on grand auto theft plus other outstanding warrants. A Washington criminal history report revealed he was a class C felon for theft, bad checks, fraud, and probation violations. A bench warrant was issued for him.

Hoover went to the state patrol office and told them of the man's activities. He showed troopers the criminal history report. Hoover joked that he could make a citizen's arrest and detain the man, but that he thought he was getting a little too old for that. The troopers said, "No, don't do that! We will take care of this." They asked when the man was to meet with his client, and Hoover responded that it was today at 2 p.m. They asked whether Hoover would be there, and he said yes. So they exchanged cell phone numbers and they said they will call or you can call us. They said they would be in the field.

Hoover drove his vehicle to the north side of the restaurant and lounge and set up surveillance. At 1:45 p.m. the trooper called him and asked whether the suspect was there yet. He was not. Hoover said he would call them when he arrived. He then got a call from his female client who asked if he was there. She said the man had sneaked up to the building on the south side, unobserved. Hoover notified the state trooper. Everything was a go.

Hoover's client pulled her car into the parking lot adjacent to the man's Ford Explorer. Hoover's vehicle remained parked away from the man's. Per instructions, the client went into the restaurant and met the subject in the lounge. They sat at a table and ordered mixed drinks. The state trooper instructed Hoover to go to the entrance door. The troopers arrived and met him at the door. They discussed the situation and reported that they had just received a computer report that the man was driving a stolen vehicle. They asked Hoover to lead them into the restaurant and point out the man and woman so they could apprehend him.

Hoover walked inside, down a narrow hall and into the lounge. He pointed out the couple as they talked at a table on the right side. The troopers approached the table from the right and left sides. The man looked up at them as they asked him to verify his name. He did. They asked him to stand and place his hands behind his back. They placed handcuffs on his wrists.

Hoover's client asked what's going on, what did you do? The trooper responded that he was being arrested for driving a stolen vehicle plus outstanding warrants. The man replied, "It looks like I have been had."

He was escorted outside to the trooper's vehicle and searched. Troopers also searched the Ford Explorer and found a German Sheppard inside. The dog jumped all over the subject who asked if he could take his dog with him. The troopers refused and called for the Humane Society to take the dog. Inside the Explorer, troopers also found extra vehicle plates and clothing.

The subject was taken to jail. Hoover's client was satisfied, but still fearful of what would happen if the man came back. She had a hand gun and knew how to use it. If he returned to do her bodily harm, she would use it. She also had relatives living close by her 80-acre plot, a family owned property that had been in her family for 200 years. Case closed.

The Naked Truth About Private Sector PIs

Note: the "naked truth" means bare, truthful information. It is a term used in the professional private investigations and security field.

The first thing a person must do who wants to hire a local, successful private investigator or the world's greatest private investigator is to discard all the preconceptions learned from television series or the movies on private investigators or 007 secret agent James Bond.

Hoover grew up in Tacoma and has extensive experience being an investigative specialist. He previously served a tour in the U.S. Air Force and sought a law enforcement career. He ended up in the private sector.

Private investigators did have a cloud over their reputation to the average citizen. They had an impression that was left by cases being solved within 30 minutes or an hour. A PI is usually a tough individual who won physical fights or shoot outs. When asked how fictional PIs from books, movies, or television compare to real PIs, they answer that the portrayal is not accurate. Anyone remembering a famous, fictional PI who was a tough, hard-fisted street fighter has a wrong impression of real PIs. The idea that PIs are surrounded by rich beautiful women with whom they have sexual involvement is in reality a no-no. Professional ethics require morals and scruples be maintained in a highly professional manner.

Average clients don't usually say, "Money is no object." Real PIs do not match the fictional detectives on television or movies or books. Today's PIs are professional, well educated people with high ethical standards. Most have knowledge and have been trained in electronics, computers, electronic counter-measures, covert cameras, tracking devices, and electronic surveillance.

The Hoover Agency's specialists handle all phases of investigations and intelligence gathering. They have local, national, and worldwide contacts. They have over 40+ years of experience in the private sector handling corporate, industrial, undercover operations, thefts, drugs, espionage, sabotage, security analysis, executive protection, security, protection, and electronic counter-measures and debugging.

In the private sector, a PI can become a millionaire, but the average investigator or agency just makes a living. The very large agencies and security firms with great success end up with very high profits.

The average PI who begins in the field of private investigations faces a maintenance financial status trying to stay in the business for a long period of time. To survive in business, you must be good – the best. Never leave a stone unturned. You need a good reputation, morals, ethics, and you must be able to adapt to cases and ever-changing laws, rules regulations, and equipment. When gathering intelligence, you must dig deep, keep on digging until you obtain the results.

There will always be a need for a good private investigator no matter what happens in the future.

PIs such as Sherlock Holmes and Watson are almost a thing of the past. However the need for puzzle solving and finding physical evidence remains the same. There is still a need for good old detective procedures, but today we have the assistance of computers, crime labs, DNA, etc. We use high-tech equipment such as GPS systems for tracking packages, people, and vehicles. We use covert cameras to document evidence and catch subjects. Physical surveillance requires the utmost patience because of the long hours and many dull moments.

There are many security firms which have private investigators on their staffs. Many of these security giants provide investigative services and are owned by ex-law enforcement personnel.

There are PIs in the Tacoma-Seattle area who worked for a security agency known as Pinkerton. The term "private eye" was derived from that agency. One agent, Dashiel Hammett, worked with the agency for eight years. He worked on various cases in the great Pacific Northwest. He later became a fictional detective writer. In 1926, Hammett, 23, tailed a suspect. He was ambushed and hit on the head with a brick. Until the day he died in 1961, he bore the indentation of the brick on his skull. There are hazards PIs face working on certain cases. They must be on their toes.

Hammett paid homage to the invaluable experiences he had as a PI in the great Pacific Northwest area. He had a Tacoma connection to one PI who had been associated with Hoover Investigations for many years. He worked in insurance sales and then entered the private sector as a PI. He was later taken under the wing of an attorney and became a national figure in criminal trial and personal injury cases. He specialized in personal injury cases with this attorney and assisted in other investigation. He utilized the Hoover Agency for information, tracking witnesses, and domestic cases.

The attorney was a special person. He was 44 year of age and his in-house PI worked for him for about 10 years until he died in 1981. The attorney helped many people but never complained. He had a very good outlook on life. He felt there was a solution to everything. He served on the bar association and helped the community with various services. Even though he was very busy, his time seemed unlimited. He handled nationally-recognized cases with some of the nation's top attorneys.

He successfully defended one client in Hawaii in a marijuana smuggling operation. The opposing attorney was famous and nationally-known F. Lee Bailey. Bailey, prior to becoming an attorney, was a PI himself. He was adamant about the use of private investigators. He relied on evidence gathered by a PI when going into court. The legal profession relies on PIs.

During the Nixon presidency, one person was wanted on federal charges for planting bugs (electronic transmitter listening devices) on political opponents and on various charges of break-ins of offices in the White House, Watergate, and in Washington DC. Upon his apprehension, he said he did it to help the people of our country and our government. He thought it would help our president.

He went to prison. But while there, he managed to devise and plant bugs throughout the prison. Upon his release, he became well known in private industry because he was a master of espionage. He cashed in on that notoriety by becoming a movie star and even had a television series to boot. His knowledge of spy techniques allowed him to go forward in the private sector. While he could not become a PI because he was a convicted felon, he formed an agency under his wife's name. They took in a partner. Their business boomed in private investigations and security because the man was a master in the profession of spying. They opened branch offices under franchise arrangements. Their stock bloomed. He became a spy consultant. Basically, their agency specialized in industrial counter-espionage and executive protection using sophisticated bugging detection and prevention.

Another person with the makings of a professional PI was a young man in Texas who had lost his hands and became a famous investigator. His real life relates in a way to the toys shown on TV and in movies, such as James Bond. He wore pincher hooks for hands. However, they were disguised with artificial hands. He could put his fist through a door or wall. In on hand there is a built in .22-caliber gun that fires when he flexes his muscles. He uses facial disguises on some cases too. He really has no handicap in his profession. His cases become solved. He has enough electronic technology, equipment, and fire power to make the imaginary James Bond shake in his boots.

He uses a chauffeured limousine equipped with hidden video cameras. It can see 17 blocks in all directions around the vehicle on the TV monitor mounted in the back seat. The vehicle is bullet proof, bomb proof, and has a variety of telephones. His home has a 20-foot wall around it equipped with alarms and cameras. Inside the plush residence are security devices, steel doors, weapons, books, a bar, desk, and TV monitor which show the entire grounds. His clients are mostly wealthy, and he doesn't handle general public cases. He said he's not like the six-million-dollar man, a TV character. He wants people to know how he really is. Medical advances have made him what he really is. One day, there may be a bionic man or woman.

An un-named professional in the PI field, who investigated political persons, homicides, and performed body-guard services with the Hoover Agency, later became a famous attorney in Washington, DC.

Another successful Texan was involved with famous investigations, bank frauds, and the Noriega case. He was a nationally known PI known for his legal investigative skills.

One of Hoover's personal contacts in Des Moines, Iowa, became executive editor of an internationally known newsletter for private investigators. He is also an expert in electronic counter measures.

Investigative Legal Process Serving

Investigator Hoover was called one day by a law firm's attorney. He met with the attorney in his beautiful Puget Sound waterfront Tacoma office. The attorney said he had a nice, big, rambler rental home in the south end of town. It was in good shape and managed by a realtor. The recent renter had let his monthly rent payments slide for months on end and was finally evicted.

After he had moved out, the attorney said he inspected the home and found the home's interior a mess. It was trashed, with holes punched by fists in the walls and burn holes in the new expensive rug. There was drug paraphernalia left about and the floor was covered with semen. It appeared the house had been used as a prostitute's sex den and drug house. He wanted the renter tracked down and served with legal papers.

Hoover obtained the subject's name, date of birth, description, and last known address. He obtained background information that revealed an extensive criminal history. The crimes included homicide, burglary, armed robbery, and assaults.

His most current address revealed that the man was living at the address of his father, mother, and brother. They all had criminal histories. They lived on the hilltop, a crime-ridden area of town.

Hoover began surveillance on the home, and after several days, observed the subject at his parent's house. He devised a safe and secure plan to serve the legal papers on the man. He placed them in a disguised large brown envelope that looked like an official parcel with an enclosed check. He attached a postal certificate to the envelope that required his signature.

During the final surveillance, Hoover observed the subject in the house. He parked in front of the fenced yard that had a walkway leading to the wooden front porch and the living room door. He got out of the car and continued approaching the house with extreme caution. He saw two men sitting by the front door on the porch railing, talking to one another. With the envelope in hand at the front porch, Hoover knocked on the door, but the two men said nothing. An unidentified male came to the door. Hoover asked for the subject by name. The man replied, "No, man, he's not here and he don't live here and we don't know where he is."

Hoover said he had a special delivery for him. The men on the porch kept eye-balling the envelope, practically burning a hole through it. Hoover did an about face and left the porch. As he passed the men, he heard one whisper to the other, "It looks like a check."

Hoover approached the gate when he heard a yell, "I'm your guy."

Hoover went back and met him on the porch. He fit the description he had: he was 6'-2", 300 pounds. He signed the receipt, using the name of the subject in question. Hoover made a bee line to his car. As he began to drive away, he looked at the man. His face was filled with hate and anger as he read the papers. He was pissed. He clinched his fist at the investigator as he left the area. The papers had been served. The attorney proceeded to get court proceedings rolling and the man was summoned to court. Case closed.

Pre-Surveillance Investigations

These investigative work-ups are done to prepare the file for cost-effective use of surveillance. The purpose is to:

1. Make certain the claimant is in residence at the address given, and is not away on vacation or hospitalized.

2. Scout the neighborhood, identify the house, and give the surveillance supervisor the logistical information necessary to prepare the case for surveillance.

3. Establish or verify the physical description, and ascertain the vehicle description and license plate numbers.

4. Determine if there are any other persons living in the house who may be mistaken for the claimant.

5. See if there are any leads or other pieces of information that will assist the surveillance team and determine if the subject is active or working.

6. Determine in advance if two surveillance vehicles are necessary, in order to allow the investigators to get permission for their use.

A preliminary investigation is a critical component for an effective investigation.

Methods, Techniques,
and Technology Used by Specialists

There are new, advanced technology, electronics, and surveillance methods used by investigators which include common sense techniques. Surveillance is used for criminal, insurance-fraud, domestic, and medical malpractice cases, etc.

It can be a physical stake out with a camera – either in hand or hidden and covert. The camera provides proof of activities, and photographs include a date and time notation. Photography done discretely provides documented evidence needed. Surveillance is useful when used with other techniques. The investigator needs to know how to hide himself or the camera to obtain results. Skill and experience are a must. A seasoned investigator has the skills to perform surveillance by foot, in a vehicle, inside or outside, with high technology cameras ready to roll, even by air.

Surveillance requires a lot of waiting. Patience is a must. One must blend in with the surroundings to be out of sight and out of mind. Preparation and skill allow the experienced investigator to use advanced technology and electronics.

For example, Hoover and his agents analyze a surveillance situation and prepare for it. They first identify their subject – the target. They photograph him or her up close then with a wide angle shot of the activities. They must be prepared for vehicle surveillance in hot or cold weather. In hot weather, air for ventilation or an air conditioning unit are needed, as are refrigerator for drinks and snacks. In cold weather, a portable heater or warm clothes or blanket are used. Sometimes an investigator will use a hot/cold refrigeration unit to keep snacks hot or cold according to the weather.

Long surveillances also can require a portable toilet or a jar to relieve one's self. You may sit for hours on end. Your eyes need to always be focused on the target. You can't take your eyes away to read. Your body must be in physically good shape. Both your mind and body must be ready to act. You must know your environment and surroundings. At times, an investigator must play his hunches – your gut feelings.

As you sit and wait, tension and stress build. You must relax as much as possible. Stretching your body and flexing your muscles helps keep you loose and ready to act. You must utilize your mind to keep concentrated on the subject or target. You think of all the possibilities that may happen so that when the time comes to act, you are ready.

You must be aware of your surroundings and what's going on around you. When the camera rolls, it begins documenting time and place of activities. Successful results are rewarding to investigators, and so is the money.

Investigators can use a high-tech surveillance van or SUV that is equipped with a good video camera that can pan in and out to record subjects. You first shoot a close up and then pan out to record activities. The cameral is usually mounted on a tripod that can be moved about within the vehicle. Some vans use a periscope system from a roof vent for 360-degree recording. Most surveillance vehicles have dark tinted windows with a dark interior. Night vision attachments are used for night-time surveillance to see into total darkness. A GPS unit can also be used to track a vehicle and know exactly where it is at all times. When a target begins to move, you respond quickly by being on your toes. Your blood begins to boil and the heart pumps very fast and your nerves tingle. You feel the tension as it happens. Adrenalin moves you onwards, releasing your highest level of body power. It is not an easy task – just hard work, basically. But surveillance video is worth its weight in gold if you have successfully completed your assignment.

There is a proven theory used by investigators when you don't have your target's vehicle wired up with a GPS unit. When you lose sight of your target's vehicle while following in your own surveillance vehicle, you search in the direction of the last sighting. It is more than likely that the target vehicle turned. Statistics show that the vehicle made a right hand turn 85% of the time. In 7% of the cases the vehicle turned left, 6% it went straight, and in 2% of the time it parked. Those statistics may help re-establish a visual contact with a lost subject. However, if the target makes a right turn and then continues making right-hand turns or zigzags left and right or makes a U-turn, it is likely that you have been burned and could lose sight of the vehicle. When that happens, it is appropriate to break off the surveillance quickly and disappear. Take it up a few days down the road.

A less expensive vehicle tracking unit than a GPS is called "the Bumper Beeper." It is a transmitting device hidden on the vehicle just like the GPS unit, but it transmits out a beep to the surveillance vehicle's receiver/monitor. It also shows the direction the car is traveling and when it turns. There is a 180-degree unit, but the best is the 360-degree unit.

There is also another unit that tracks telephone cells. As with the GPS, it uses satellites. Reel-to-reel GPS units use a lap top computer to keep you on top of your target. Movements are shown on the computer screen. It shows location, time and speed. It can also be printed out.

The telephone cell unit can only be located on your target within a cell site. Once the target has been located, surveillance can be conducted. The Bumper-Beeper 360-degree unit is the oldest and is still used in maintaining continuity of the target vehicle. It can be coupled with the other units if desired. It radiates a signal from the hidden transmitter on the vehicle to a decoded compute-receiver. It develops timing synchronization signals from the transmitter. It gives horizontal and vertical SNC pulses that are very accurate and show the direction of the vehicle in a crosshair on the screen.

Covert video equipment and tracking units are a very discrete method to keep track of one's activities. Video cameras can capture photos of activities within a dwelling or an area. The video camera with a transmitter and receiving monitor attached to a VCR can record activities from miles away. A video system can also be attached to a telephone line so activities can be monitored and taped on a VCR thousands of miles away. Wireless systems and telephone link systems have become more and more like equipment shown on James Bond 007 movies.

Insurance fraud and disability claims require surveillance to prove or disprove deception. There are 10 points to consider:
   1. Excessive demands
   2. Soft-tissue injury/prolonged
   3. Self-employed or family-owned business
   4. Leads from co-workers, neighbors or competitors
   5. Known history of malingering injuries
   6. No present organic basis for complaint
   7. Subject looking for early retirement
   8. Disability occurred just before lay off period
   9. Subject never home to receive telephone calls
   10. A gut feeling or a woman's intuition

With all the technology today, with its methods and techniques, and with more technology coming in the future, there's a need for specialist investigators. There are many types. The Hoover Agency has used many specialists through the years. There are many types of investigations. The kind of specialist needed depends on what kind of case you have. Some specialties include:

Arson investigators – determine whether the cause of a fire is natural or arson. They determine how the fire started and who would benefit from the loss.

Background specialists – investigators who look in depth into the background of an individual

Bilingual specialists – an expert interrogator who has skills to question a person in a foreign language

Ballistics experts – people who examine firearms, matching bullets to a particular firearm

Bounty hunters – locate and retrieve people who skip bail when released from jail on bond

Chemists of geology – analyze soils for safety and human factors

Closed circuit TV specialists – experts who install covert cameras for inside and outside surveillance

Credit fraud specialists – who track persons to prove fraud for prosecutors

Computer technology specialists – who investigate computer fraud or other cyber crimes. They track them down and prove the case for prosecution. They examine computer hard drives for evidence. They provide analysis to show where a person has been on the internet. An online sting operation may be set up to catch the person.

Criminal forensic technician – analyzes evidence brought into the lab. May be called into the field to obtain physical evidence in a homicide.

Document examiners – prove documents are valid by analyzing handwriting, typewriters, and other type of equipment

Drug/narcotics experts – who prove by analysis a substance is in fact illegal

Electronic counter-measure specialists – provide a service to eliminate all electronic listening devices (debugging). They provide methods and devices for countering transmitters that invade their space.

Environmental specialists – investigators who determine any and all EPA violations or chemicals being dumped

Explosives investigators – detect and defuse bombs, gather evidence for the case

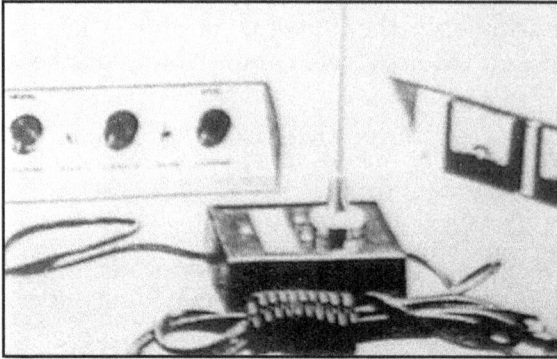

The "bumper beeper" vehicle tracking device produces 360-degree, all-around signals

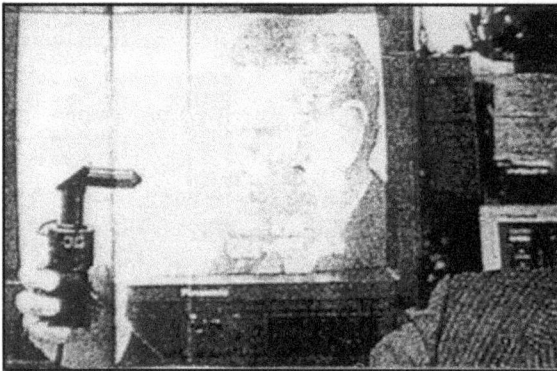

A video pin-hole camera

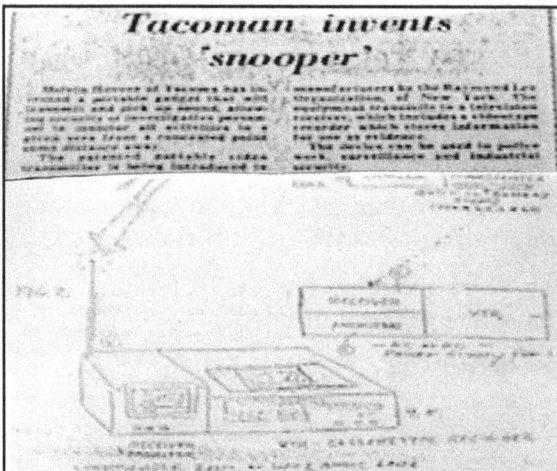

"Inventor" Mel Hoover's diagram of a wireless covert video system in 1974, reported in the Tacoma News Tribune. Hoover patented the system, but lost rights to an electronic security corporation which manufactures the units now in use by law enforcement. The electronic technology has become more refined over the years.

128

Financial investigators – CPAs determine if fraud, embezzlement, money-laundering, diverting of funds, or skimming has taken place for arrest and prosecution

Fingerprint technician – to dust for and lift prints plus photograph and analyze comparison prints. They fumigate an object or use another method to obtain prints.

Forensic specialists – pathologists who perform lab analysis of chemistry, DNA, and dentistry to identify persons by teeth or to compare teeth with bite marks on criminal cases

Ghost investigators – use electronic equipment and cameras to analyze and inspect to determine if a dwelling may have a ghostly problem

Insurance investigators – obtain finance fraud or injury accident evidence. May require surveillance from a surveillance specialist

Laboratory technicians – analyze human body factors such as hair, toe, hair, DNA

Marine specialists – investigate and analyze accidents on vessels

Marital/child custody experts – they know the type of evidence needed to document the case. They use photography to help document abuse, drugs, the environment pertaining to the health and welfare of children.

Mechanical engineers – analyze a mechanical problem, such as metallurgy, corrosion, elevators, tire mishaps, or other mechanical devices

Meth specialists – determine illegal chemicals have been manufactured in a building. Environmental cleanup is required by the owner for safety of people who come back into the area. Note: some Washington counties contain one of the highest meth-making concentrations in the United States. There are clean-up specialists trained and certified for the state. Many companies are now providing clean-up services for home owners. Hoover's youngest son and daughter-in-law own a clandestine meth clean-up operation. They are Jerry and Corinna Hoover of American Environmental.

Missing person specialist – one who can track down and locate adults or children. Some can be found by computer searches. Others need physical tracking. Abductions and runaways require investigations.

Nuclear investigators – scientists dealing with nuclear substances. They investigate the presence of nuclear substances used in making a bomb. May locate and dispose of the same. They help determine whether there is any espionage or theft of nuclear secrets.

Polygraph and PSE technician – determines the truth to a degree. It depends on the years of experience to obtain good results. Polygraphs have been beaten by a very few people in past years.

Process servers – locate and take legal steps to serve legal documents on people. Must be able to skip-trace. Hard cases require an investigation to locate a person and serve them. They may also do collections.

Surveillance specialist – requires patience and endurance to know how to surveil a person by foot, vehicle, air, boat, train, bus, or by closed circuit television. Covert cameras and video photography record one's activities, within the legal means of the investigation.

Vehicle accident reconstruction specialists – reconstruct auto crashes to find the cause and liability in accidents

Voice print technicians – analyze voices, compares and matches them using recording equipment. May enhance or refurbish a recorded voice tape, including surveillance video.

Many of these methods, techniques, and technology are used by investigators who are specialists, whether in law enforcement or in the private sector as security personnel or PIs. If they are not a specialist and need one for a case, they call one to get results they need. Some PI agencies have their own specialist personnel, and many are retired detectives, FBI agents, and CIA agents.

There are new methods and advanced techniques being borne as this book is being written. The technology of electronic gadgets soars to battle crime and to convict criminals who tend to scam with existing technology. Specialists must stay current and counter with even newer technology in the future to catch and prosecute the criminals.

Note: Law enforcement and private investigators may be certified specialists qualified to perform many of these tasks during an investigation. If unqualified, be sure to call a specialist.

Note: Another specialist in need at times is a locksmith. Mary's brother and sister-in-law, Jim and Shirley, are locksmiths. They operate White Knight Locksmiths, in Auburn, Washington. Jim had a locksmith business in Mississippi, where he worked with many law enforcement agencies, helping to apprehend criminals.

Father Jim Ebeling Sr. served in World War II and Korea. Wife Mabel supported his efforts – from Private to a retired officer (Major) with the US Engineering Corp. Jim became a specialist for Bank of California as a security vault attendant – 35 years military service, 20 years with the Bank of California.

Corporate Investigative Giants

The Hoover Agency has been involved with some corporate investigations for businesses in Pierce County. Hoover never became a corporate investigative giant, but dealt with some corporate investigative giants throughout the years. Their political ties helped them excel in that world. The future of corporate investigations throughout the world will be very demanding and financially rewarding.

The Pinkerton Detective Agency was established back in the 1900's when the private sector was born and expanded out west. The agency was virtually unchallenged until 1909. During this time, the Justice Department established the Bureau of Investigation, known as the FBI. Later, another agency began Pinkerton, with a trade mark still known today. "The eye that never sleeps" is a phrase used by private investigators/agencies throughout the world. The statement makes it clear that they are in business as investigators, keeping a sharp eye out for their clients, day or night. The Allan Pinkerton Agency is one of the oldest private detective agencies around. It immigrated to America in 1842 from Scotland. Pinkerton joined a police force and by accident formed his agency. The agency specializes in corporate investigations and security.

The Hoover Agency was established in 1964 and is one of the oldest agencies in Pierce County. It has completed assignments nationally and around the world.

During Mr. Pinkerton's time, a newcomer established an investigative agency. In about three months of business, William J. Burns took one of Pinkerton's most prized clients away from them, the American Bankers Association. In 1888, Burns was 30 and a US secret agent. He investigated federal land frauds and performed political investigations. Through the years, the agency was passed on to family members as was the case in Pinkerton's, as well. Their offices expanded nation wide. Their business took in well over $200 million annually and employed 40,000 people. Half or more of them worked full time. The agencies performed investigations and security. The detective assignments comprised only a small fraction of their revenues. The biggest portion was in security.

The third largest giant in this field of private investigator firms is the Wackenhut Corporation. It was established in 1954 and was originally known as Special Investigations Inc. The owner, George Wackenhut, was a former FBI agent. The company was based in Miami, Florida. Most investigators handling the cases were ex-FBI agents and security guards. Some were ex-cops.

Today, investigative giants have grown in numbers and with branches stretched throughout the United States. They investigate corporate crimes and provide security for corporations. The high demand for those services has created a booming industry raking in billions of dollars annually. Since the 9-11 incident, the movement of terrorists into and within America has boosted business far into the future. Security is now a must. Companies are also demanding that investigators work to provide reports on their competitors.

The Hoover Agency has investigated various businesses and has provided reports regarding business competitors. There are some people out there who are not investigators who use illegal electronic listening devices on competitors. They then sell that information. These people are known as corporate spies. They use a variety of methods and techniques to obtain information. Therefore, the corporate world has a need for debugging specialists who locate eavesdropping transmitters. The Hoover Agency has done electronic sweeps for various businesses and individuals seeking out those hidden transmitters in cars, homes, on phones and on people.

Then there are the terrorists and other foreign people in America spying on us daily by electronic means. They tap into computers and intercept communications. Therefore, the corporate world is seeking good security measures to protect and secure their world from competitors and enemies to ensure secure operations.

Spies have been spying since the beginning of time, and it is on the rise in the USA. These spies, some of whom are foreign double agents, sell information to foreigners.

Investigators who do corporate investigations will excel in the future. It is not only because of the 9-11 incident, when terrorists flew airplanes into our World Trade Center in New York, killing thousands of people.

Corporations want to be safe and to prevent spies from gathering intelligence regarding their businesses – information on their financial status or their products. They don't want it sold to competitors.

The US government should have been tracking foreigners since day one. You know that if J. Edgar Hoover was still alive and still the FBI director, 9-11 wouldn't have occurred. He'd have been tracking those foreigners every step of the way. Foreigners in America move about freely and answer to no one. They go wherever they want to. They do what they want.

About 20 years ago, the Hoover Agency gathered some intelligence from people in the CIA and FBI. Their knowledge even back then was that the terrorists will strike America – it was just a matter of time. It's just like when Pearl Harbor was attacked by Japan on Dec. 7. The government was informed then, too, but just let it happen. The same with 9-11. Foreign and domestic spies in the USA gathered intelligence top secrets that they sold for the sake of money. That information could destroy America's way of life through chemical or nuclear sabotage and destruction. Terrorist groups have been gathering information for years on our way of life. That's how the 9-11 plan worked so quickly. Terrorists use fear and death and destruction. They themselves do not fear death. They'd rather look death in the eye and take as many American lives as possible.

America must be safe and secure for our families. Therefore, security measures are a must for corporations and the government. We are so free that advocates have used that freedom to weaken our laws. Punishments need to be updated to fit the crimes. A spy could possibly get 10-15 years, a murderer 7 years to life. Foreigners in America become citizens and then become public officials, representatives, and politicians. They can then distort and hollow the US Constitution. You can see it when issues are manipulated by our representatives in various levels of government.

Private Investigators Abroad

The Hoover investigative agency has done business with various investigative agencies in the US and abroad. We have given assignments to PI agencies abroad, and they, in turn, have used our agency for work in the USA. Having foreign resources to call on and using them for your clients can be very profitable. However, it must be handled properly. You must know each other's backgrounds, such as years in business, their licensing status, and their reputations. The firms need to establish good communications between themselves. The hourly rates and expenses must be known, a limit established, and then foreign currency exchange rate factored in.

After making contact with an initial contact person, a written agreement must be agreed to. You must make sure your contact person speaks English, and the report must be written in English. The contract or agreement between the two firms must specify that a good written report be in English. It is also good to know whether the foreign agency is a member of a reputable international investigation organization so that if there is a problem or claim, it can be resolved with assistance of that organization rather than resorting to legal action.

Agencies need to clarify their rates, enumerate expenses, and set a maximum allowable amount in a specified currency. Firms should allow at least a 20% inter-agency commission based on billable time, not expenses. Their agreement should specify that a precise billing and detailed expense listing be provided with written reports so that domestic firms can provide the same for their clients.

When assignments are received or given out, they must include as many details about the case as possible. Details such as the target subject's name, address, good physical description along with a photograph, age, height, weight, build, race, hair color and style, complexion, glasses, clothing, facial hair, jewelry, unusual features, voice, accent, how he walks and talks, and the use of hands to stroke the nose or hair should be provided. You should include as much background on the case as possible. A time limit for the investigation should be established and dates set for receipt of a complete written report. The agreement should also specify how the report should be transmitted, such as by Federal Express, United Parcel Service, or fax.

In yester-years, the image of PIs abroad used to include the traditional brimmed hat and trench coat

To aide communications, investigators should exchange information about how to make personal contact, specifying the time, dates, phone numbers, office hours, holidays, weekend and after-hours numbers, and the time zones. Firms should make surer the assignment can be done on schedule, and that should be confirmed in writing.

American agencies should explain to their clients the cost of the international investigation and the problems that could arise, such as more time may be needed. They should collect large retainer fees to account for those factors. Of course the American agency should have a contract with their client that specifies the approximate time needed to complete the investigation.

International investigations can be performed relatively easily with a good profit margin if you use professionals, have good communications, an agreement, and work together. It will bring about a successful investigation with less cost to the client.

The image of private investigators, such as old Sherlock Holmes, with the old trench coat and brimmed hat, came from European countries. This famous Sherlock detective image drifted to the United States and to the movies. So a private eye image was created. Humphrey Bogart, a famous actor, traditionally wore the brimmed hat and the trench coat in his detective movies. Once those images came, they were copied by private detectives in the United States.

Today, however, attire worn by investigators at home and abroad has changed. The entire profession has changed into professional investigative and security agencies. As previously mentioned, Allan Pinkerton brought professionalism to the industry. He and his people opened their agency in Chicago and became very successful. That success has been extended into the new millennium with branch agencies throughout the United States.

One famous private investigator abroad during the 1840s was Francois Eugene Vidog, He established the first agency in Paris, France. As agencies grew in the US, they also grew in Europe, England, and other Anglo-Saxon countries. It was a rough go for them to succeed because they were suppressed by totalitarian governments for nearly half a century. However, they finally excelled as they did in the USA. It took a while because of the wars and communism.

American investigators began to use European investigators for investigations abroad, and visa versa. Associations were established in the US and abroad. Two of them are the Association of British Investigators (ABI) and the Council of British Investigators (CII).

Detective agencies have expanded into many European countries and even into Asia, Mexico, Canada, Africa, Norway, and Ireland.

The World Association of Detectives is a great association for contacting professional investigators world-wide.

While the backgrounds of American and European detectives differ, the exchange of investigation assignments with agencies overseas has changed the status of service so that it is possible to obtain an investigation anywhere. The world has become so small in reality, both with our rapid air travel and the use of worldwide information networks that provide contacts for business or pleasure. Investigators can use the computer to locate someone or track assets in fraud situations. But to verify findings, investigators still need a physical presence on the ground.

In the United States, there are claims that crime is down. Yet look around you. There is murder after murder, theft after theft, and large corporate, white-collar crime. The iron curtain around Russia is gone, and when it disappeared, crime rose to no end. The American-Russian mafia spilled into the United States with drugs, thefts, and prostitution along with other scams. There are other foreigners in the USA who have formed their own mafia too. These criminals, such as the Muslim terrorists responsible for 9-11, and Mexican gangs, moved very freely about.

In the next chapter we will cover art theft in this country. Art thefts go hand-in-hand with criminal drug, fraud, and prostitution activities. Art can be used as collateral for the purchase of illegal drugs. The drug lords buy art from illegal art sales. It has become an exorbitantly lucrative field. The soaring prices for great world art – paintings, sculptures, and artifacts – has made art a target for thieves. It is known as the second largest international crime. Number one is narcotics and drug trafficking. Drug lords usually launder their dirty money, and one way is through art deals. Art is then transported from one country to another.

Law enforcement officials believe that criminals are art oriented. They are usually high caliber individuals who dress and speak well. However, they are very dangerous. They do not hesitate to murder anyone who gets in their way. When they move on a target, if guards or police working for private art collectors cross their path, they are history. If employed, these people steal from their employers and swindle the art collector or dealer. They are classified as "art nappers." They may also shoplift a painting or small bronze sculpture. As in other crimes, there is always a fence man, or middle man, who disposes of the art and takes 10% of its value in return. That person locates buyers, possibly art galleries, and sells the art.

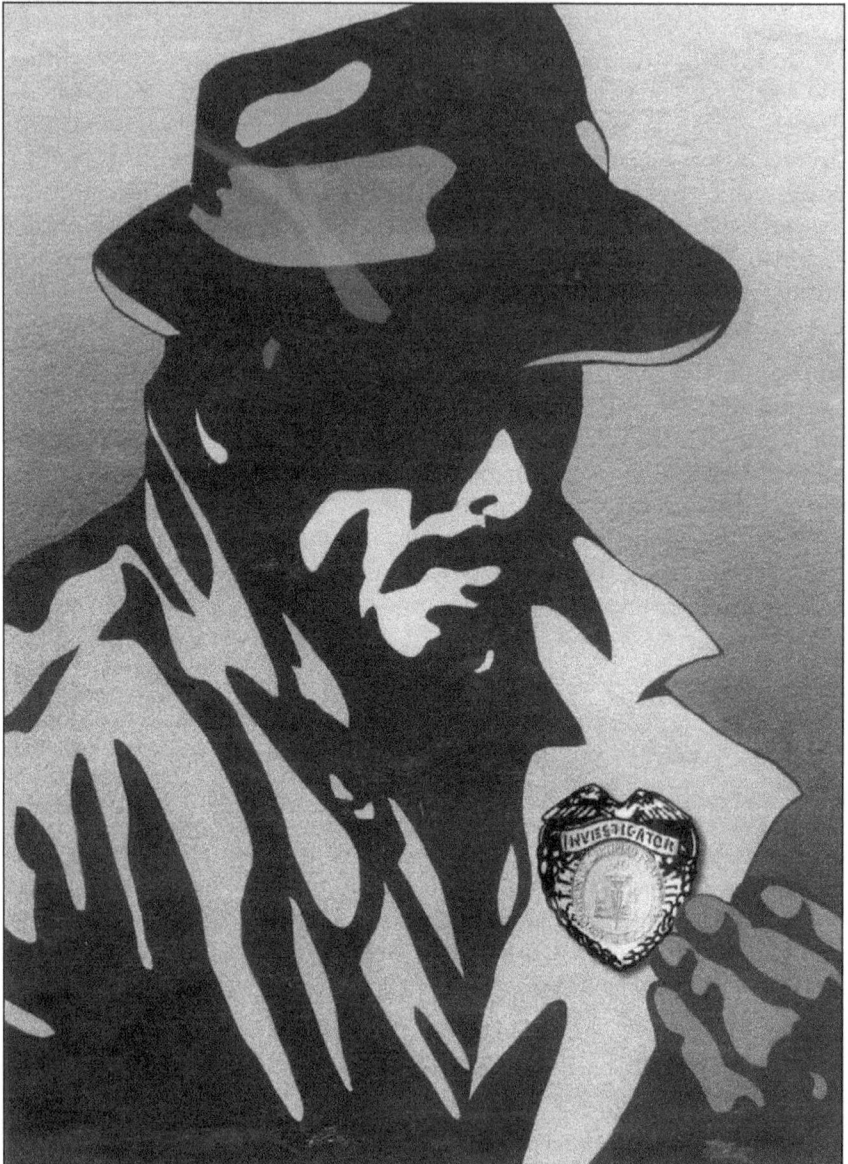

Drawing of a "PI" investigator in USA. Image stemmed from abroad, trench coat and brimmed hat

Worldwide Art Thefts

Investigator Mel Hoover has dealt with art theft cases. He researched art thefts around the world. The world is full of beautiful, famous art created in the past or present. They include drawings from artists dead or living. The high-class paintings leave the door open to the world of thieves. There have been many valuable paintings stolen through the years. The FBI has taken note of the cases once brought to their attention and it established a computerized index of stolen international art work. Before that, it was done manually. But the computerized records were placed in the NCIC (National information Center.) It includes detailed documentation of current and past stolen art that allow a match up to be made that could lead to suspects and an investigation of them. Recoveries and arrests are more possible with this system in place.

In the private sector, private detective agencies working on art theft cases can work hand-in-hand with the FBI. Since 1991, there have been more than 30,000 art thefts in New York City alone. That is when the FBI entered the picture by indexing and computerizing the thefts. Now national and international thefts are being interlinked with law enforcement agencies worldwide. Art dealers and various agencies indexes the art work to control and track them to names and faces. Then, when a theft occurs, they can zoom in on a party in question.

Investigators should obtain a theft report showing the victims' name, address, phone number, name of the artist, title of the art work, and the type of work, such as canvas oil painting or oil on wood panel or pastel watercolor. The description of the artwork should also include its size listing the vertical dimension first. Whether the artist's signature was on the work and where is also important information, as are any other identifying marks. The report should also identify when and where the theft occurred and who was associated with the piece during showings or transport. The report should also list the name and phone of the person receiving the report as well as insurance information. A photo of the art work is also needed, and it is helpful to know if there is a reward for the return of the piece.

Art thieves are very sophisticated specialists in their trade. Some are hit, run, smash, and grab practitioners, while others plan and inside job. Investigators around the world, too, have become very professional and specialized in art theft cases. The backgrounds of United States' private investigators in this field differ from that of their counterparts in Europe and other countries. While there may be some likenesses, the overseas detectives are connected to the police and military which gives them the power of enhanced information and services. There are many retired investigators and detectives and law enforcement personnel who enter into the private investigations field in the US.

As an example of background requirements for European private investigators, those in Belgium must acquire a 5-year college degree in criminology. The Belgium parliament enacted the requirement in 1992. Spain, Austria, Germany, Italy, and France require 3 years of university criminology study.

Stolen art work has been known to find its way to various parts of the world. Therefore, investigators must become more and more professional. They must be tested and licensed as knowing the rules regulations of the field. Associations regulating the field require more knowledge and training in relationships with clients and various fields. The Federation of Detectives exists throughout Europe and includes about 15 countries, including Israel, Greece and Portugal. Germany has the IKD, the International Komission Fur Detektive-Verbande. The World Association of Detectives is the largest international association in the world. It is established in the USA and on the European continent. In Europe, it is mainly Italians and the British. It includes Asian and South Pacific countries. Associations provide more education in the field and state and world-wide contacts. They upgrade the private sector by laying down rules, regulations, and education requirements that maintain professionalism in the private sector of investigation and security.

The world has become very small in reality. There are state-to-state contacts with agencies in the USA doing exchange business abroad. Investigations can be performed anywhere and at any time with less cost to clients; anything from locating a stolen piece of art work to finding a loved one. "You can run but you cannot hide!"

Worldwide art thieves also sell to antique shops or restorers or attempt to slip works through an auction house sale. Illegal trades people buy or sell stolen art. A survey in 37 countries confirmed the information. Trades people with stolen art transfer ownership illicitly. Thefts occur in public and private places where there is insufficient security protection and where there is no system of technical protections. Security is a must and it must be planned to protect the artworks. Certain security programs have been enacted. Theft of art had been ignored by law enforcement. However, the FBI saw the problem of art theft in the USA. It appointed specialist detectives to investigate art thefts. There are a few private detective agencies such as the Hoover Agency which have been called upon to investigate art thefts.

An investigator must have techniques and knowledge of art history, the art market, and know people in art circles. An investigator should know how to identify art works and be able to recognize fraudulent art. Contacts with US and foreign underworld informants are needed. An investigator should have knowledge of the art community itself.

People dealing in art work should have a good record-keeping system that includes markings on pieces, where they have been displayed, the dates in and out, transportation details. These are good protective measures. An investigator should be trained about art and involved with and knowledgeable about the art community such as museums, universities, auction houses, and art associations. The investigator must also have on hand very qualified art persons to assist and instruct. Having all of these ducks in a row should help an investigator produce good results.

Collectors, dealers, and museum administrators must follow certain precautions to protect themselves from purchasing false or stolen art. They should make and receive theft reports to inform individuals of complete descriptions of stolen art.

Industry contacts include:

1. National stolen art file, Lab Division, Document Section, FBI, Washington DC 20535. Telephone: 202-324-4434. Interpol c/o US Department of Justice, Washington DC 20530. Telephone: 202-739-2876.

2. FBI; Interstate Transportation of Stolen Property Squad, 26 Federal Plaza, New York, NY 10278. Telephone: 212-335-2700

3. Commanding officer, Property and Recovery Squad, New York City Police Department, 1 Plaza, New York, NY, 10038. Telephone: 212-374-3823

4. US Treasury Department, New York, NY 10048 Room 410K Team 203,6. Telephone: 212-466-5500 ext. 5709

5. International Foundation For Art Research Inc., 46 E. 70th St, New York, NY 10021. Telephone: 212-879-1780

6. Art Dealers Association of America, 575 Madison Ave., New York, NY, 10022. Telephone: 212-940-8590

7. National Central Interpol, Cultural Property Unit, 1200 Alta Vista Dr., Ottawa, Ontario, Canada K1AOR2 0101. Telephone: 613-993-3232

8. Auction houses in area notify largest Sothebys, 1334 York Ave., New York, NY, 10021. Telephone: 212-606-7000. Christies, 502 Park Ave., New York, NY, 10022. Telephone: 212-546-1000. Phillips, 406 E. 79th, New York, NY, 10021. Telephone: 212-570-4830

Drug Lords and the Mafia

Drug lords from abroad and in and out of the United States involve governments, such as our FBI and CIA, and their political ties. The drug industry is a multi-billion dollar operation. Will the world's drug problem be eliminated? I don't think so. There are just too many people making money off drugs. Some are investors, others are the drug lords. Drug lords stem from many countries, including the United States.

It is a chain reaction – like a snowball rolling down hill. So many people tend to fall under the drug lords. Basically, it is money and greed and power trips that take them over. It furnishes them a nice, expensive home, boats, exotic cars, limos, and very large bank accounts. They don't care that people using the drugs destroy their lives or die. It is their bag to obtain tons of green backs. A drug lord or any person dealing drugs is basically a murderer. However, the greedy ones jump on the band wagon. These are the investors who double or maybe triple their investments. Do they care about the people hooked on drugs? Of course not! The investors could be politicians, lawyers, doctors, movie stars, producers, etc. Maybe they are also a distributor or dealer and possibly hooked themselves. It is a big scene in Hollywood. Performers, producers, rock stars, princes, Playboy center-folds, and magazine writers. Each fall into that rolling snowball web of drugs and corruption. The mighty dollar is the goal as is the addiction to power and greed that destroys so many people's lives.

Immigrant foreigners from abroad have formed mafia-like gangs that have no regard for life. They will take you out in a blink of an eye. We have the Russian mafia, Asian mafia, Mexican/Cuban mafia, etc. The Cubans play a big part in distributing drugs. Columbians who distribute kilos net $750,000 and more per year. Our government today and in the past deals with other governments, exchanging information or whatever, and allows drugs to enter the US. They make deals with the FBI and CIA. Fighting drugs is a futile battle, a no-win situation. It makes a lot of good people go bad – policemen and the like.

We cry for citizen involvement to combat crime and drugs, but the battle continues on and on. Yes, involvement helps. But the war on drugs continues on and on with no end in sight. It will never end until our government does its part. It must end deals with other governments and begin working together to end growing and production of drugs for export. Look at drug cartels involving Castro, Bush, the treacherous Noriega, and the CIA. Peek at the Noriega files. It stems back to a cover up of our government during the Carter and Kennedy administration days. Castro and the mafia worked hand-in-hand and targeted President Kennedy. He was assassinated years ago. In a survey, 70% of the general public felt it was a conspiracy. Many investigators investigated his killing. All evidence was eliminated. Oswald was killed by Jack Ruby and Ruby died in jail. As shown by the facts of the investigation, the investigation was handled poorly and was inaccurate. CIA and FBI files were lost, omitted, and deleted. It leaves a mark on the American government. Drug lords in America are spreading death and mafia gangs, destroying lives and profiting on drugs in America today.

Foreigners in the United States move freely about using cars, public and private aircraft, and boats. Many others sneak into the country bring in kilos of cocaine. It's a multi-billion dollar industry with the mafia, drug lords and government involvement. Drugs flow state to states as mafia members worldwide flow into America. Some are terrorists waiting to destroy the American way of life. Government and private investigators and the news media have investigated various mafia crimes of drugs. The mafia gangs work with drug lords, money laundering, prostitution, white-collar crime, corporate and computer/cyber crime, gambling – they all go hand in hand.

The original Italian mafia has been around for centuries. Now, in the new millennium, it no longer stems from just Italy. It is a disease that has spread to many cultures. They have landed in the good old USA; Japan, Columbia, Mexico, Brazil, Russia, Samoa. They are big drug businesses with drug lords selling drugs and weapons, and prostitutes. They are very dangerous people who kill in a heart beat. They snuff out a person's breath in seconds and think nothing of it.

It is a world-wide movement and it has targeted America. Our government is helping them to destroy us from within. Our late director of the FBI was a tough guy; tough on crime and criminals. He kept tabs on everything and everyone in the US. He died very mysteriously and was discredited after his death because of his personal life style. J. Edgar Hoover warned America before he died to stop the drugs coming to America before it takes us over. Do you think he was right or wrong?

No one listened to him. Too many people were involved in making large sums of money. So greed and corruption prevailed. No one listened and no one is listening still. They're not seeing what is going on. It has destroyed a lot of young people's lives and the drugs have caused numerous deaths and murders of Americans. Our laws are weak and foreigners know it. Murderers get a slap on the hand usually. We need tough laws to fit the crimes. If you are a convicted drug lord or dealer, you should be executed.

No one really likes to take a life, but they would take ours in a heart beat. Terrorists take these stands and use death and fear to excel. The same goes for the drug lords and dealers. They're excelling in the booming business of drugs. Law enforcement is fighting an uphill battle and will be for years and years to come. There are too many advocates – do-gooders – not wanting to take anyone's life.

Let's stop the revolving door of the justice system. Save America and save American lives. The corruption of the all-mighty dollar is destroying America from within. It involves people in very high places. People seem to turn their backs on God and their constitutional responsibilities. Therefore, they are selfish, greedy, immoral, permissive people who have become no good to society.

The criminal element is growing and has produced violent criminals with disregard for human life. There are good foreigners, as in every walk of life. But crimes are on the rise and terrorists plot to do America in. The working class is paying the freight with taxes for jails and federal prisons. But unjust laws protect criminals' rights. What about victims' rights? They deserve fair and swift trials for criminal with punishment fitting the crime. There is racial tension growing within the country, however there are foreigners in high public offices. We the people seem to be loosing control of our government and laws that could convict and punish criminals.

Today's mafia, of which there are many now in America, are pouring in tons of various drugs and are making money by the tons. Some are, in fact, supporting terrorists financially. Mafia figures are defrauding people through white-collar crimes, medical rip-offs, billing schemes, medicines, and buying and selling body parts. Identity theft has come into play; stealing ones identity to make a huge profit. Some of those criminals have ties with drugs and gangs. It once again shows that crime pays for the criminals, not the victims.

Have we lost control of America's destiny? As previously stated, there are many foreigners in high government positions and offices. So there are leaders today who are not Americans in today's society.

Hotel, Motel Security

There are people who travel and use hotels and motels who feel they are safe because of various security measures that these establishments supposedly have. In fact, surveys throughout the United States on hotels and motels show security is lax and fails to perform the necessary security and fails to use methods and procedures. So it is safe to say that most of your hotels and motels are unsafe.

Criminals can portray themselves as maintenance men or janitors or maids and perform burglary and theft with no problem. He or she can obtain valuables from the rooms. A man observing a woman alone can contact her room by phone. Using a pretext, he can claim there is a problem in the room that needs fixing. Once personal contact is made at the door, he can enter and assault, rape, rob, or kill her.

A homicide with an assault, rape and robbery took place in a well-established nationally hotel. A couple, feeling secure, received a phone call from a maintenance man claiming there was a problem with the fire alarm in their room. He was given an ok to come in and make repairs. The couple did not call the desk to verify whether the call was true or false. Once inside, the man assaulted the husband, beating him with a hand gun until he was dead. He then assaulted the wife, raping and robbing her. He left the room unnoticed and unheard.

National investigative surveys show it is easy to gain access to rooms without being observed. Using various pretexts, people obtain room keys from the front desk. Sometimes, closed circuit cameras are not operating. Other times, perpetrators use a distraction method - accomplices to fool those monitoring cameras. People use side or rear doors to enter, and use parking areas near entrances to enter/exit without being noticed. At times they even use the main entrance with no problem.

Hotels and motels obtain much damage and are insecure most of the time. Sometimes, there is outside extra security. However, internal thefts within the rooms occur. People steal or make keys for the rooms. Lots of time housekeepers steal or are involved in theft rings, drugs, prostitution activities, or meth labs. There are housekeepers who are honest, reliable, hard workers. Yet some slip into being thieves since their wages are low and their tips minimal. So temptation becomes a factor. But then there are good and bad people in all walks of life.

146

Hotels and motels have a tough time surviving and have numerous ups and downs, profits and losses. Management that employs security 100% of the time and provides their clients good service in safe, protected rooms should improve their profit margin.

In the criminal's eye, the hotels and motels which are very lax are trying to save money. Hotels and motels with good room service and a safe environment will excel in the long run. The cons see hotels/motels as easy prey. They are able to obtain what they want – sex, money, valuables, and so on – without being detected.

The hotel, motel business nationwide is striving to be number one in service and profit. But some are lax and are targeted by criminals because they are lax with security procedures.

"Hotel"

LODGING

Threat of Terrorism and the World of Spies

Terrorism often appears to be unpredictable and even irrational to its victims. But terrorists are usually rational individuals who use terror tactics to achieve their goals. Most use fear and death. Some, such as those in the Middle East, use religious basis to have their people achieve their goals. They target businesses, government, officials, structures, water and food supplies, etc. They use physical forces of bombings, chemical and biological warfare to disable businesses to inflict financial hurt on government and its people. Some are media savvy and want to be recognized for their actions as a way to achieve their goals. They instill fear in the people to force them to meet their demands. They operate low-key in one- or two-man teams or more. They spread out about various locations in the world. They visit countries and reside as common fold, the friendly next door neighbor, waiting to move in on their targets for complete destruction. They work in underground networks so law enforcement is unable to infiltrate them. But their targets are well planned and they execute their mission to achieve their objectives. There are terrorists worldwide recruiting people of different nationalities to become terrorists.

People in the Middle East countries have been living with religious problems since time began. Killings and bombing happen day to day. Those tactics are ways to achieve their goals. Life doesn't' mean a thing to them. They are honored to use their life to kill as many of their targets as possible. The mid-eastern terrorists have had their eye on America since our government became involved there. Middle East problems are widespread and the terrorists are becoming stronger. In some respects, there will be no rest over there. Problems will continue with more fighting and wars.

The Hoover Agency had contact with a retired CIA agent 15 years ago who was interviewed for a private investigator position. During discussion about terrorists and their targets, he said that the United States would be attacked – that it was just a matter of time. Violence would be against the perceived power structures in the US – government and industry and its people. The government let the matter slide. It bought no precautions or security measures to protect America. Foreigners move in and out of the US with their activities and objectives unknown. In a free country, people move about very freely doing what they want to with no questions asked. The terrorists within the US did the same. There are terrorist cells within the US,

Terrorists use kidnappings, extortion, and bombings as part of Theory "F,"
for fear and death.

Canada, Mexico, and other countries. It is a worldwide problem. All countries need to cooperate to eliminate terrorist activities.

There were some measures taken against particular individuals – security check lists. Individuals who may be targets of terrorist attacks must be alert to the very real potential problem. These intimidating, coercive acts are criminal; kidnappings, bombings, sabotage, assassination, extortion. A political movement is needed to persuade the population and government that specific political and social changes must occur.

The characteristics common of most terrorist acts include:

1. Violence method of systematic persuasion
2. Selection of targets/victims with maximum propaganda value
3. The use of un-provoked attacks
4. Selection of acts to gain maximum publicity with minimum risk
5. Use of surprise to overcome counter measures
6. Threats of harassment, violence that create an atmosphere of fear and death
7. Lack recognition of civilians/women/children
8. Use of propaganda and maximum violence to achieve political/economic goals
9. The perpetration of terrorist acts by groups whose only loyalty is to each other

Terrorists spy on many of their objectives and then plan their attacks on targets.

As an example, the Sept. 11, 2001 attack on the World Trade Center in New York was planned years in advance. The spying and planning paid off in the destruction of a great structure, killing thousands of people and hurting the US mentality physically and financially. Now we're in a battle to eliminate all terrorists, yet they're everywhere, seeded in our world in various countries ready to act on command. Security and defense for the American people will be costly from now on. Countries are in need to ban and rid these forces of evil from the earth. Fear and death plagues us all now. We never know where they will strike again. Just like the 9-11 attack in New York, terrorism has caused havoc on our economy which was already hurting. They are striving to break us financially, and it appears to be working. Look at our national debt since the war in Iraq.

The terrorist spies will always be there, a threat to us all in the future of the world. The blame lies on lax American security. No one wanted to face the issues to spend money on security measures and investigating foreigners flowing into America. There are many spies in the USA from many various countries. Just like the mafia gangs, it all goes hand in hand. The airlines and our government had knowledge that hijackings had occurred. Really, no steps were taken to tighten security with airlines. No air marshals or other security measures were used. Airlines could have done a lot themselves, but no one wanted to spend money. It was pushed aside and the gambling wheel spun around. When it stopped on that red dot, we lost. So we were late in our nation's security. Now the war will continue for years to come. It's a war hard to win, just like the drug wars we face today. Allies need to work together to prevail.

American freedom is very precious, and we have become united as a nation once again. It took the terrorist spies to make it happen. There should be standards of protection to prevent this from happening again. Should we let foreigners come into America and roam about freely as American citizens?

As we know, our world is full of spies, and there are many within the US. There are some in high places who would sell secrets, as seen on the news. Everyone is vulnerable to the threat of spies. They are using electronic invasion devices. There have been surveys in the past in Western Europe and the United States that determined there are well over 200,000 bugs (electronic listening devices) planted year after year. Government and corporate spying has been accelerating. Corporations spy to beat the competition. The electronic invasion consumes one's privacy in all sectors of life.

In US spy shops and private investigation agencies, the use of electronic gadgets has been growing for years. There have been newspaper headlines in the New York Times, the Boston Globe, and Forbes such as, "US warns on threats of wiretaps," or "company alleges wiretaps by ex-v.p.," or FBI bugged by hi-tech, bug proof telephones," or "deals made on bugged US Moscow embassy." The best defense against corporate espionage is counterspy techniques. Electronic snooping is not just for the spies. Business is booming. "Bugs for You! Live and Lets Spy!"

Businesses are selected as targets for various reasons. They may be for take-over plans, for buying/selling computer programs, to learn marketing strategies, etc. Governments also spy on one another to have the upper hand in case of war. Terrorists plan their moves of death and fear to achieve their gains in the political world.

Business and government alerts against electronic eavesdropping:

1. Where are you most vulnerable in your dwelling for listening devices or wiretaps to be placed?

2. How could an adversary easily crack into your computer and access code data?

3. How secure is private, personal conversations in dwelling telephones against clandestine transmitters on concealed frequencies? How should these security problems be handled to prevent any type of clandestine eavesdropping?

Who would want to bug you?

1. Anyone who wants knowledge of your personal or business data and documents. Bugs can be made or purchased for as little as $30 and usually only takes seconds to install to obtain valuable information on products, equipment, secret data, etc.

2. How do you know you're bugged? There's no simple answer to secure your private conversations. Rooms can be bugged, telephones tapped.

Government and business and some individuals need privacy. Every situation needs analyzing to determine whether to pursue security measures.

1. Determine the level of perceived threat

2. Personal, local, regional, or national level

3. Type information targets want to obtain

4. Persons of question who may be involved and their financial resources

5. How should information be protected and how long

6. Determine countermeasure equipment to keep communications secure.

Once a threat level has been determined, one must determine the type of countermeasure equipment available to meet or exceed the perceived threat. Electronic countermeasure devices used in periodical debugging sweeps can defeat the threat levels and assure safe, secure conversations, data, and information.

Financial information may be at stake, or competitor information, union information. Even employees may want to obtain information and sell it to competitors or brokers. Secret information in aircraft, auto industry, or the government may be sold for many dollars, even millions. Remember, information can also come from faxes, computers, and telephones. They can intercept wireless computers to steal your identity, your bank account, etc.

WHAT IS INTERPOL ?

The International Criminal Police Organization, is better known by its radio description – Interpol.

- 136 countries are members.

- General Secretariat is at St. Cloud (Paris) France.

- Annual General Assembly is hosted by a member country each year. This is attended by the top police/enforcement officials of member countries.

- Symposiums occur almost monthly in various countries, attacking particular crimes by given geographical area, or worldwide.

- NO INTERNATIONAL LAW as each country maintains its own sovereignty and operates within its country's law only.

J. Edgar Hoover and the JFK Conspiracy

The world of spies and terrorism strikes leads to many political ties throughout the world. As we look back into our government and the present happenings, there's reasonable doubt about our government's actions. The late J. Edgar Hoover, director of the FBI, was respected by some in the political world and feared by others during his career. Individuals were profiled by Hoover and many others. In his 48 years of service, he devoted his life to the profession for, basically, America's freedom. He started the very first police academy and the federal agency. He became known as a man being number one in leadership.

John Edgar Hoover is credited with making the initials FBI. It has remained a symbol with the agency to date. Hoover was a man of integrity and stood tall because the politicians did not control or own him. In our present time, there is political control of most police departments in the US. Hoover was feared by politicians and by criminals, including the mafia. He established the academy training. It was strict, rigorous. It had methods to select the best men for the job and they were given the best training to fight crime.

Hoover was known to resist all crimes and all criminal forces out there. He died a mysterious death in which there appeared to be a cover up by the US government. Hoover mentioned there were foreigners in and out of the US who were out to destroy us. He knew drugs were a main factor in the plot to destroy us from within. They would destroy our basic structures of society.

Presently, it has been happening. Drugs are everywhere in our society. Are we saying NO to drugs? They are in our education system, on our streets, and within most main major cities. They create a loss of control. The downer of drugs creates educational havoc, shootings, and the rise of racial problems. Hoover could have stopped these evil forces. He saw it coming, and our government just let it happen.

Hoover made many statements before his death to which no one apparently listened. He said, "America should take note before it is too late or one day we will face chaos." The problem is beyond the point to correct today, but as Hoover stated, it could be controlled. "Our fight against crime can be no stronger than the courage and commitment of our citizens," he said. More of the finest police officers will not bring about control of today's crimes.

JFK

Oswald

Ruby

Hoover was an idol and benefited by some of his traits, beliefs, and power to combat crime without being politically controlled. He had the knowledge to see what was going to happen and the need to correct it for the future.

Documents in FBI files revealed Hoover was concerned about the image of the FBI. He kept files even on fictional celebrities and actors, such as the British agent 007, James Bond. Bond movies, such as Goldfinger, showed women in scanty attire. They were very beautiful. Therefore, the FBI investigated since the movie contained three passing references to the FBI. A confidential memo stated that the book, written by Ian Fleming, was not the type of movie in which the feds wanted to be portrayed. Even if the federal agents looked favorable in the movie, Fleming stories centered around sex and bizarre situations. He could not imagine that the FBI wanted to be associated with Goldfinger. The investigation was groundless. Old Hoover was always on top of everything and particularly if it involved crime or the agency. So James Bond was able to save the gold and Fort Knox with only the help of the CIA and the US Army, not the FBI.

During the presidency of John F. Kennedy, Hoover had his eye on Cuba and Castro. Castro was dealing with the mafia in the US, making drug deals and other things. Castro was considered to be one of the world's most dangerous men during these times. Cuba, under communism, had various ties with the Russian government and Vietnam during the war. After the Bay of Pigs, there was a plot to kill President Kennedy since he was against drugs and crimes and was coming down hard on them.

Later, President Kennedy was assassinated. Hoover had knowledge that there was a plot to murder the president. It was being investigated and originated in Chicago and Miami. Ties with the mafia in Illinois and Florida were with Fidel Castro, known as the Bay of Pigs. Then there was some evidence that some authorities in New Orleans knew of the Dallas assassination plot before it ever took place. There was also an indication the vice president, Lyndon B. Johnson, knew about the plot in which there was another twist. There was the possibility of a plot of murder with conspiracy ties involving the Marilyn Monroe, who was involved with Kennedy in the past.

Hoover had some prime suspects who he believed were involved in the plot. The mafia mob had reason for the murder or murderers to get rid of the president and his brother – because they were too hard on criminal activities, especially the mafia. They were involved in drugs, the civil rights movement, and the Vietnam War. They also had ties to Castro and his people. Criminal interests, backed by right wing groups and big businesses, the billionaires, were losing business and money, because of the FBI and CIA. It appeared to all be tied with the Bay of Pigs during the Cuban missile crisis.

The president spoke about having a big stick (atom bomb) and was ready to use it if necessary. Kennedy was coming down hard on all of these people. Therefore, a plot was laid to kill him. All these people involved wanted him gone. The plot was a well-planned conspiracy to kill the president. They had in place scapegoats to take the fall and for witnesses or ties to be eliminated. There would be no available witnesses to talk, ever. Some of these big business people, probably the billionaires, paid large sums of money to do what was needed without knowledge of what or who set the whole thing up or any of the details. So there would never be a connection to any person or persons.

The assassination of the president of the United States, John F. Kennedy, who basically was for the low and working class people in America, was to happen because he wanted to combat crime and criminals. He was trying to protect and save the country for future Americans and to have a better, safer place for the children of our American society, just like J. Edgar Hoover.

That fatal day came when a shot or shots rang out, supposedly by Oswald, a Russian trained sniper with his Russian sniper rifle, in Dallas, Texas. Oswald was caught in the building with the rifle and it had been fired. However, there were other shots coming from the grassy knoll observed by witnesses. They observed a man or men behind a fence on top of the knoll firing shots. White puffs of smoke and the smell of bun powder was evident. It is a fact that shots rang out from the top of the knoll. But witnesses were harassed and threatened. There was a man who had movie film of the event. The film was taken from his camera. There was another person who took pictures with a still camera, and that film was also taken by authorities. These witnesses were classified as silent lambs, and there was no one who came forward witnessing the event. Every one of the witnesses with or without a camera was in great fear for their own lives.

It boiled down to a government cover-up, a conspiracy to assassinate the president.

Oswald was trained in intelligence work in Russia. He was on the 6th floor where he fired the rifle from a window in the school book depository building. There were witnesses who noted the shooting.

When arrested and escorted from the building, Oswald stated, "I did not kill anyone." But a film was obtained that showed the shot coming from the 6th floor window.

Later, Oswald was conveniently escorted unprotected into a crowd where Mr. Ruby walked right up to him and shot him point blank with a 38 caliber revolver, killing Mr. Oswald right on the spot. It appeared to be a professional hit. His lips were forever sealed. Ruby, the shooter, was a nightclub owner nearby. He was involved with organized crime figures, the mafia. There was a contact between the two before the shooting of Oswald. Ruby was placed in jail but conveniently became ill and died before any interrogations began.

Paraffin tests could have proven whether Oswald had fired the shot. But there were a number of mix ups of evidence. There was also an observation that two rifles were removed from the building. One was caught on film being brought down the back fire escape. The other came out the front door with Oswald. Empty shell casings were found, but were fingerprints taken? There was another man wounded during the assassination.

This conspiracy within our government can be classified as the cover up of the century. There was a gunman or gunmen on top of the grassy knoll, according to witnesses. But disinformation and misinformation was planted involving a Clancy Holt and Rosco White.

Audio tape recordings of Oswald were found that have been analyzed by the reverse speech process to reveal the truth or deception. This was backed up with physical stress testing later. It was also backed up by further PSE testing. It proved that Oswald didn't really assassinate the president.

Investigation into the assassination of the president involved many top-notch investigators. Experts in the field had many theories. Many sided with government rulings that Oswald killed the president and that there were no other shooters. The entire pro and con boils down to many unanswered questions, many missing links, and unsupported ties among the information provided.

Conspiracies have been part of government since the very beginning of governments. Things are buried and forgotten in time. People move on with death and the lives of a new generation spring forth. Nobody knows anything. It is done and forgotten once there is no evidence to pursue. So time and people change, and the conspiracies are forgotten.

Many investigators believe in their research and the investigations that were performed. That is true of the Hoover investigative agency. There was a cover up. There is no way to prove it once all the evidence and witnesses are gone so conveniently. The CIA knows how to do that very well. Many of our foreign enemies have specialized organizations that can assassinate and leave no clue as to who did it. The assassination of President John F. Kennedy and Kennedy family members were political, very well planned, and were later covered up. Various investigations were revealed to the public. Some people bought them, others forgot them. However, the investigations revealed reasonable doubt in most investigators' minds.

Many of the investigators didn't like the end results. There was reasonable doubt because so many things happened and how they happened. It kind of snow-balled, beginning with the mysterious death of the director of the FBI, J. Edgar Hoover, then President Kennedy, and next, Senator Bobby Kennedy who was running for president. Then there was the connection with movie star Marilyn Monroe. Was her death a suicide? Maybe it was a homicide. Monroe had knowledge of what was going on. More than likely she knew of the assassination plot to kill the president. Vice President Johnson may have had the same knowledge and may have been involved. No one will ever know the truth. You see, there was always the process of elimination of the true evidence. In every one of these cases, there exists an explosion, and encyclopedia, of many mysterious missing links.

The conspiracy theories are one of many in governments. Another example of a cover up was when George Bush was president. Later came Bill Clinton, and then came the son, George Bush Jr. If you look at all these cases, there is reasonable doubt. No true answers will be provided.

Director Hoover's mysterious death was swift and silent. It was given no exposure to the public. It was swept under the rug very quickly. He was buried and that was the end of it.

Then there was the assassination of President John Kennedy and his brother after him. Investigations left reasonable doubts in most Americans' minds, including the death of Marilyn Monroe.

Then came President George Bush who convinced the American people that someone else made the mistakes: Oliver North. However, President Bush, the commander in chief, gave orders down the chain of command. There were various cartel drug deals involving the CIA, Oliver North, the mafia, Castro, and Mr. Noriega. These very, very treacherous links and dealings with the United States by North, who just obeyed orders, made him the scapegoat for the president. Can you call this a cover up or a conspiracy in the making?

Then came President Clinton and the scandal about this personal life. It may have been a set up. Was this another conspiracy?

Thereafter, George Bush Jr., the son of the former President Bush, ran for president. His brother was governor in Florida. When the voting came about in Florida, there was a question of rigged votes for Bush. There was an internal look into the matter, and then it was dropped. Could this have been a cover up and a conspiracy?

John Kennedy Jr. and his wife took off in a small airplane. He was the son of President John F. Kennedy who was assassinated years ago. The junior Kennedy was the little boy at the time who people saw on TV viewing his father's funeral and who saluted to say goodbye for all America to see. He was an up-coming candidate possibly to run for president. His small plane crashed in the sea. There were no survivors. It leaves a question in one's mind. Was he targeted and killed knowing he'd become president one day? It is a question for thought. This could have been another cover up and a conspiracy in the making for a long, long while.

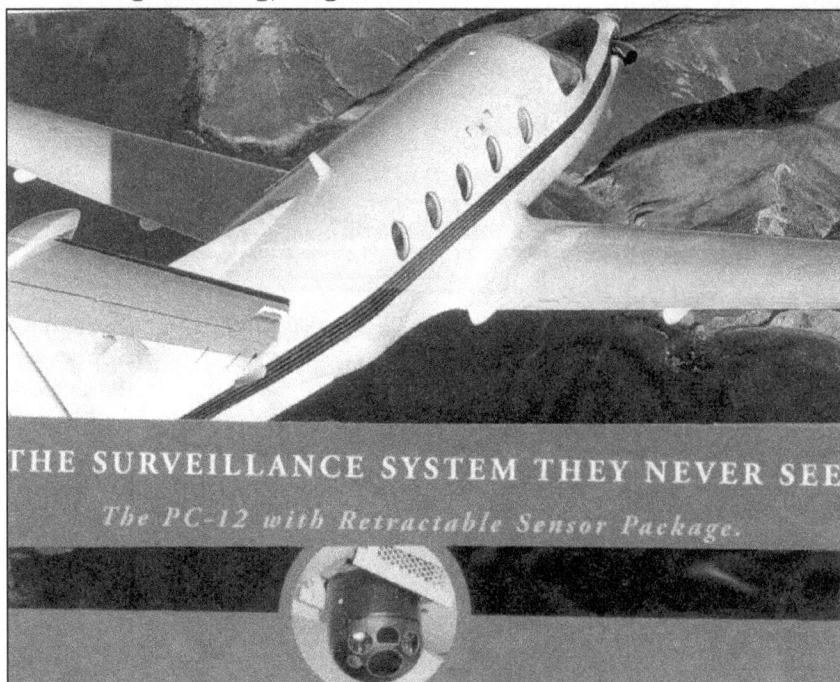

THE SURVEILLANCE SYSTEM THEY NEVER SEE
The PC-12 with Retractable Sensor Package.

Surveillance by Air

Forces of Evil

Evil lurks in man and about the world. For example, what makes serial killers? It has become a nationwide issue. They strike at random and are usually unnoticed by anyone.

Several serial killers have been at large in the great northwest. One was in King County's Seattle, Washington. He is known as the "Green River killer." He killed mainly street walkers, prostitutes, around the Seattle-Tacoma airport. Women were picked up by a vehicle and transported to a remote area. He sexually tortured and raped them, then killed them. Their bodies were dumped by the Green River. This is how the label "Green River killer" came about.

Numerous women were killed using the same method of operation (MO). There was one woman survivor who had been sexually assaulted then stabbed numerous times and left by the road for dead. She managed to make her way to the road side after the killer left. As luck would have it, she was found by a person driving by who saved her life. Police worked with her after her recovery attempting to identify the killer. A profile was developed and a general description composite drawing was made. It wasn't conclusive.

The Hoover Agency was called by one of the victim's relatives to investigate leads on a volunteer basis. Leads were followed up and interviews of people showed no links or suspects in particular after many hours of volunteer investigating. Yet there was one person fitting the description shown on the drawing. He was a local man in the community who had a family and a good job. He usually went out at nights in a suspicious nature. Information was turned over the Green River police task force team. This killer was usually one step ahead of law enforcement agencies. He knew when and how to strike when the coast was clear.

Surveillance was begun on this subject and he was stopped by patrol units in the Sea-Tac Airport area. The police ran a background check on him which showed an involvement with street walkers. They later interrogated him. Search warrants turned up no hard evidence linking him to the killings and he was released. Many thought that the police had over-reacted. However, years later, with additional surveillance by police, he was again picked up. They obtained a DNA sample from him and released him. Then DNA was obtained from victims and matches were made that showed that in fact he was the Green River killer. He was once again arrested and charged for numerous murders.

The evil forces of serial killers have risen throughout the United States. They kill at random, selecting their targets and usually picking up their victims off the streets, unnoticed by passers by. Victims are taken to remote areas, tortured and raped and killed. What really makes these people tick? It is the evil within man himself, a twisted perverted mind. Yet they are very smart to cover up his dual life and killings.

The forces of evil are out there and will remain out there. Just like people who are involved in ritualistic cults or terrorism – they go hand in hand. There has been an alarming increase in ritualistic crimes in America. There has been evidence of murders, animal sacrifices, sexual abuse of many children, and occult-related suicides.

Investigations by law enforcement and private investigators have found ritualistic occults involving Satanism and drugs. The investigations consist of their criminal activities and association with the drugs used in their occult practices. Law enforcement and private investigators focusing on these issues are training and learning about Satanism and ritualistic activities. Basically, occult activities involve teenagers at different levels, such as use of heavy metal music albums centered on occult themes and lyrics and symbols, all associating with drugs.

Note: Occultism is not by itself illegal, regardless of the practitioner's age. However, when crimes are committed as part of the practice, or drugs are used, it is illegal.

Levels of Involvement in Occult Practices

Fun and games. People at this level usually are non believers just involved to get peer acceptance. No participation in group rituals is involved and they don't have knowledge or terminology of ritualistic occult practices. The activities consist of playing heavy metal music with satanic lyrics or playing theme games such as dungeons and dragons.

Dabblers. People interested in reading literature and collecting paraphernalia such as witches, knives, chalices, incense, bells, gongs, candles, etc. These people use the terminology, participate in the rituals, and are easily influenced in group activities. Then they feel justified to commit crimes.

True believers. Adults and teenagers accept the ideology as you would any religion, such as Protestantism or Judaism. They use the tenants of the occult as spiritual, moral, and ethical guidelines in their lives.

Ritualistic criminals. Usually teenage dabblers and adult true believers who have taken occult religion to the extreme. Crimes include trespassing, vandalism, theft, cruelty to animals, kidnapping, sexual abuse, rape, murder. At the crime scene look for alters, candles, chalices, biblical verses written in blood, listings of ritualistic dates, symbols such as the inverted cross pentagram, 666, natas, and so forth. Sexual activities fixate on anal abuse, goat heads (symbolizing the devil) or animal mutilations.

So, many forces of evil strike out in our world as investigators learn and train in this special investigational field to resolve crimes.

The following are some occult terminology for reference:

Alter – main ritual room

Black magic – uses of powders of evil purpose

Blood – part of man which survives death. Drinking it, you acquire traits of a person with divine qualities

Circle – 9-foot diameter on the floor. Magic done inside for protection and strength

Coven – practicing group of 4-20 people

Degree – ranking within the organization

Ears – signify wisdom of spiritual development

Esbat – coven meeting

Evangelist – represents Satan at rituals

Finger – holds spiritual powers. Index finger is "poisoning or cursing finger." Must not use to touch a wound or it will never heal

Fire – symbolizes Satan

Heart – symbol of eternity and the seat of emotion and intellect. The hearts may be eaten to acquire characteristics of victims.

Inverted cross – mockery of Christian cross

Missal – book with rituals and teachings

Nudity – believe essential in raising forces through which magic works

Ritual – tool to focus individual power of group members on common concern subject

Sabbat – significant holidays and celebrations

Serpent – serpent with horns is symbolic of the demons

Shrine – ritual table

Sorcerers – those who have made a pact with the devil

Talisman – an object believed to hold magical powers

Warlock – male practitioner of Satanism

Water – symbolizes Christ

Witch – female practitioner of Satanism

As this wild world turns around and around, the mafia gangs grow by the numbers throughout the United States along with the religious cults. The forces of evil upon us seem to spread death and violence combining the war on terrorism. Terrorists live for violence, fear, and death for their causes. The US government in global exchanges brings about various police actions and wars. Therefore, this brings forth terrorist attacks against America and its people. Thus, there are spies everywhere.

Cults have been involved in shootouts with the Bureau of Alcohol, Tobacco and Firearms and the Department of Treasury. Terrorists, in movements to destroy America's foundation, plan hijackings of aircraft, political killings, bombings within the US and abroad. Then came the 9-11-2001 attack. Once again they hijacked aircraft on a suicide mission to kill and destroy the World Trade Center in New York. They did so by steering the planes into the building and killing thousands of innocent people while America already had a struggling economy. This really hurt us financially, with great losses to the American people in the private sector and government. There were also attempts on the White House. Airlines called for tightened security, but it was too late. It's better to be late than sorry.

So more and more security specialists have put their heads together to tighten security and provide body guard protection for the politicians, executives, etc. more and more foreigners coming to the U.S. day by day could be America's greatest downfall. Plus the drug smuggling sponsored by terrorists. Industrial espionage by foreign spies continues. Terrorists are spread throughout the world with financial backing of many countries. They have various methods of operation. The shooting of CIA headquarters in 1993 proved to be politically motivated and related to the Muslims in Bosnia.

Our nation is growing, but the forces of evil seem to expand with it. Plans of domestic terrorism, the KKK, Aryans, and Nazi skin heads are examples of right wing extremists recruited on a day-to-day basis. They are very violent convicts. Most are brain washed by a form of cult practices. Police attempt to monitor their activities if and when possible. Various religions that have been formed into cults are on the rise. They use brainwashing. Terrorism is of great concern for American people in future years, as are satanic cults that have been a well-kept secret for years. Terrorism will more than likely lead to other wars in our world. Allies, throughout the world need to band together and seek out gangs, drug lords, terrorists, and eliminate their finances. It is the only way that will stop the terror – by all going after gangs, drug lords, terrorists – we as a nation can not do it alone.

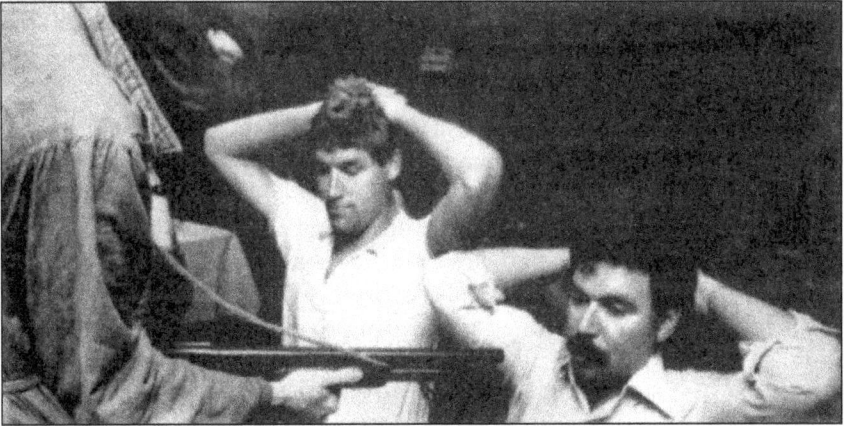

San Francisco – Learning Survival – "Terrorist" Hans Van Loos holds a shotgun to the head of television reporter Tomas Roman (right) and another unidentified "hostage" at a San Francisco hotel. Though the 1-1/ 2-hour ordeal looked and sounded real, right down to the blood and guts when one of the hostages and the terrorist was shot, it was all a mock hostage situation used by Canadian-based Eagle Anti-Terrorism and International Security to train corporate executives how to handle possible terrorist attacks.

Future of America and
Private Sector PIs and Security

Our future was predicted by the late J. Edgar Hoover, director of the FBI, and has become a reality. He warned us of the political issues that grow and take over control of the people. These politicians in control mislead other politicians towards corruption. He warned us of growing drug issues and ties with various mafias now in the US. He mentioned conspiracy plots and foreigners coming to do away with America's way of life and terrorists planning to destroy America's structure, education, and economy. They use drugs for their financial support in order to live here and attack when ready.

The future of America depends on the American people. The elected officials, the do gooders, are soft on crime. Criminals have all the rights while victims' hands are tied by laws. Politicians need to change laws to gain back control of America for the people.

Hoover said, "We face chaos." Sure enough, it has happened and is happening. 9-11 could have been prevented. No one listened. Elected officials did not accept their responsibilities. They only thought of themselves and their wallets. What has happened to God and country? The middle working class people are the backbone of America, but they are disappearing. America's future lies on the American people to stand up and make the way by voting to change laws, politicians, judges, lawyers, and to control essential factors such as food, water, electricity, gas, oil, wood, and medical care.

Beware of the terrorists who seek to destroy our needs and collapse us from within. They are using gangs, the mafia, and drugs to bring us down. So we need to be tough on crime and criminals. We need security to keep America a safe place. We need the courts to bring swift punishment to all criminals, especially to the ones who commit violent crimes. More prisons are just a burden to the American people. It is necessary to eliminate the bad from the face of the earth, to put "An eye for an eye" into practice, to make a better, safer America.

We don't like taking a life, but criminals don't hesitate to take one or more lives. In the old West, if you stole a horse, you were hung to the nearest tree. In mid-evil times, they also got rid of any evils that were a threat to their society.

We have a great government and a great country. We can prevail under God providing necessary steps are taken to preserve America for a better, brighter future for our children and grand children. We need to preserve America and stop wars unless we are threatened with destruction of our country. We need to work together with other countries to seek and destroy all terrorists.

Wars are a way to control people and to bring people together. Wars are costly and American people should come first. They should be able to have the American dream home, their family, and jobs for everyone with no poverty in the USA. This should be a goal. We need medical care for everyone, and veterans should be honored and cared for.

People need to wake up and be aware about government control, know what's happening to the American structure. American people can make a difference. We can stand united and exert pressure on political parties. We can vote and change laws, change politicians right down the line. Spending billions overseas has brought a burden to the American people and it will cost you, your children, and your grandchildren.

The future of the private sector security and private investigation industry is bright. The need for security exists because of the terrorist threats. Many crimes produce a need for more security and investigations. Frauds and scams are on the rise, and we need investigations, investigators, law enforcement and private eyes. Homicides, missing persons, computer thefts – you name it – are blooming along with a greater demand for more security. Therefore, the demand is never ending for law enforcement personnel, private investigators and security people.

News reporters interviewed Mel Hoover on several occasions about the future of the private investigator in the Northwest. Hoover said he has been in the business over 40 years. You name a case, he has done it. As one "Hoover I Spy" character said, "There will always be a need for good investigators."

There are advanced technical equipment, procedures, electronic gadgets, DNA, GPS, and computers. These are only tools of the trade to assist in solving crime. You still need a good investigator with intelligence, a mind to put together the whole puzzle. Obtaining supporting evidence and placing all the pieces of the puzzle in order solves crimes. That's what pinpoints the subject in question and establishes guilt beyond a reasonable doubt.

God bless America. Stand united. Stand tall. The American people can and will make changes for the good of the people, for the people and by the people.

Mel and Mary, "MM"

Owners & Operators
of

Hoover Professional Investigations

Tacoma, Washington
"Since 1964"